# THE
# GOLFER'S
## BOOK OF
# TRIVIA

Cover design by Designworks, Inc.

Library of Congress Catalog Card Number
85-60301
ISBN 0-933341-00-8

First printing April 1985
Second printing July 1985
Third printing November 1985
Fourth printing March 1986
Fifth printing September 1986

*Published by*
Quinlan Press, Inc.
131 Beverly Street
Boston, Massachusetts 02114

Golf is a good walk spoiled.
Mark Twain

**Wade M. Welch** is a trial attorney with a Boston firm and a two-term selectman of Winchester. A former Harvard hockey goalie, he took up golf seriously while in college in an effort to beat his fiancee, Jane; unfortunately, he picked up a case of "The Shanks" shortly after their wedding day in 1969. In spite of the heroic efforts of club pro J.L. "Tex" McReynolds, Welch has never regained the form that made him a mediocre player at the Winchester Country Club in the 1960s.

**Jane Faxon Welch,** a member of a well-known Massachusetts golf family, is a former Mass. State Junior and Junior Junior Champion. While attending Rollins College in Florida, she was invited to represent the school in the NCAAs. She is a ten-time winner of the Winchester Country Club Ladies Championship; mother of Tracy (age 15), 1985 Champion of the Mass. State Junior Juniors; 1986 Mass. State Junior and New England Jr. Miss. Champion; aunt of touring pro Brad Faxon; and wife of co-author Wade Welch.

# Table of Contents

Special Thanks To:

Reid Nelson, Public Relations Manager, Wild Dunes Beach and Raquet Club, Isle of Palms, SC

Desert Inn & Country Club, South Las Vegas, NV

Carey O'Donnell, Publicity & Promotions Manager, New Seabury of Cape Cod, New Seabury, MA

Alan T. McKenzie, Public Relations Manager, Resorts of Pinehurst, Inc., Pinehurst, NC

David S. Witter, Director of Marketing, Sea Pines Plantation Company, Hilton Head Island, SC

Sig Kaufmann, Sea Island, The Cloister, Sea Island, GA

Joe Abrams, Doral Hotel & Country Club, Miami, FL

La Costa, Carlsbad, CA

Tom Card, Dorado Beach Hotel, Dorado, PR

Ewen Gillies, Palmas del Mar, Humacao, PR

Innisbrook, Tarpon Springs, FL

The Breakers, Palm Beach, FL

Sharon H. Rowe, Assistant Manager, Public Relations, The Greenbrier, White Sulphur Springs, WV

Denise M. Adams, Manager, Radio-TV Services, Colonial Williamsburg, Williamsburg, VA

John M. Gazzola, Jr., Public Relations Director, The Homestead, Hot Springs, VA

Mike Hall, Concord Resort Hotel, Kiamesha Lake, NY

Cheryl A. Slavinsky, Public Relations Manager, Hershey Entertainment and Resort Company, Hershey, PA

PGA Tour, Sawgrass, Ponte Vedra, FL

Alexandra I. Baxley, Public Relations Assistant, Sawgrass, Ponte Vedra Beach, FL

Catherine Ollenburg, Marketing Coordinator, The Woodlands Inn, The Woodlands, TX

# QUESTIONS

# THE MAJORS

1. In the 1985 U.S. Open, runner-up T.C. Chen had two famous doubles. What were they?

2. Who lost the 1957 U.S. Women's Open by signing an incorrect score on the 4th hole, even though her 72 total was correct?

3. What is the original name of the Master's tourney founded by Bob Jones in 1934?

4. Who beat Pat Bradley in a playoff to win the 1984 Dinah Shore?

5. What club did Gene Sarazen hit for his famous double-eagle to tie Craig Wood and win the 1935 Masters? Bonus: At what golf course, and at which hole?

6. Who completed a record 27 Opens between 1937 and 1973?

7. What is the record for most strokes on a hole at the U.S. Open?

8. What do Jones, Snead, Palmer and Nicklaus all have in common about the U.S. Open?

9. In his bid for a 5th U.S. Open victory in 1955, Ben Hogan was defeated in the playoff at Olympic. Who beat him?

10. Who won the 1984 Masters by two strokes over Tom Watson?

11. Who won the 1984 British Open?

12. Who won consecutive U.S. Women's Opens in 1977 and 1978?

13. Who won the PGA Championship in four consecutive years (1924-1927)?

14. Jack Nicklaus defeated Doug Sanders in an 18-hole playoff to win the 1970 British Open. What were their scores in the playoff?

15. The winner and the runner-up at the 1965 U.S. Open were both foreign-born. Name them.

16. Between 1970 and 1983, two foreign-born players won the U.S. Open. Name them.

17. She broke four world records in the 1932 Olympics, then went on to win the U.S. Open at the Salem Country Club in 1954. Who was she? Bonus: Where and when were her other Open wins?

18.  Who was the first American to win the British Open? Bonus: How many other British Opens did he win?

19.  Jack Nicklaus holds the Major championship record at 20; what Major championship did he *not* win?

20.  Bob Jones is second in Majors at 13; what two Majors did he *not* win?

21.  Who was the first native American to win the U.S. Open?

22.  What lefthander won the British Open at Lytham in 1963?

23.  Who was the winner of the 1968 British Open at Carnoustie by two strokes over Jack Nicklaus?

24.  Who won a record six British Opens?

25.  What was the site of the U.S. Open in 1930 (which was also Bobby Jones' Grand Slam year)?

26.  Who holds the record for most Majors won by a woman?

27.  Who is the only amateur ever to win the U.S. Women's Open?

28.  Who was the winner of the first U.S. Women's Open?

29.  Name the three foreign winners of the Masters.

30. Who played in the most Masters?

31. Name the oldest Masters champ.

32. Name the youngest Masters champ.

33. Name the two golfers who won PGA Championships at age 20.

34. Who was the oldest man to win the PGA?

35. Who was the first winner of the LPGA Championship?

36. What handicapped golfer won the 1954 U.S. Open?

37. How many golfers have won two U.S. Opens on the same course?

38. Ben Hogan, Sam Snead, Walter Hagen, Lee Trevino, Andy North — of these players, who has *not* won the U.S. Open?

39. Name the only consecutive Masters winner.

40. Masters champ in 1980 and 1983, he was born in Santander, Spain. Who is he?

41. How many times did Ben Hogan win the U.S. Open?

42. What ex-caddy won the British Open with a hole-in-one on the 17th at Prestwick? Bonus: What other years

did he win the British Open?

43. How many U.S. Women's Open Championships were at match play?

44. How many times did Bobby Jones win the U.S. Open?

45. Match the golfer with his Major title:
   1. John Mahaffey          (a) 1975 U.S. Open
   2. Jerry Pate             (b) 1981 U.S. Open
   3. Hale Irwin             (c) 1979 U.S. Open
   4. David Graham           (d) 1978 PGA
   5. Lou Graham             (e) 1976 U.S. Open

46. What is the symbolic prize awarded to winners of the Masters?

47. Who was the last New Englander to win the U.S. Open?

48. What year did the PGA Championship change from match to medal play?

49. What accomplishment do Sally Sessions, Polly Riley, Betsy Rawls and Nancy Lopez share in the U.S. Women's Open Championship through the years?

50. Tom Watson, Ben Hogan, Sam Snead, Arnold Palmer, Walter Hagen — which of these players have *not* won the PGA?

51. Who apparently won and then lost the Masters on the same day in 1968?

52. In a three-year span, this Dallas native

won the Masters, two consecutive U.S. Opens and three consecutive Western Opens. Then he mysteriously "lost his swing." Who is he?

53. He won the 1959 Open at Winged Foot and the 1966 Open at Olympic on some of the world's fastest greens — yet he averaged *under 29 putts per round.* Who is he?

54. Who threw a fake snake at Jack Nicklaus while they were waiting to tee off in 1971 U.S. Open playoff?

55. Who did Francis Ouimet beat in the three-way playoff at the 1913 Open?

56. What was Bill Joe Patton's "Waterloo" in the 1954 Masters? Bonus: Who also came to grief there in 1985?

57. A natural southpaw and former Japanese softball pitcher, she won the British Women's Open in 1984. Who is she? Bonus: What was her margin of victory?

58. The site of the U.S. Open in 1940 and 1946 and the PGA in 1973, this course's 16th hole — 605-yard monster — and 14 doglegs have resulted in many double-bogies for the short hitter. Name the course.

59. Who is the first black to play in the Masters?

60. Who stopped Watson's bid for his sixth British Open win in 1984?

61. After winning, he donated all of his

1965 U.S. Open prize money to charity. Who is he?

62. How many times did Harry Vardon win the British Open?

63. Who won the first PGA Championship in 1916?

64. What was the lowest score ever in a U.S. Open?

65. Unprecedented and unequalled, he won both the U.S. and British Amateurs in consecutive years. Who is he?

66. Who scored a hole-in-one in the British Open at the age of 71?

67. What is the largest margin of victory ever in the British Open?

68. At 5'5", 137 lbs, he won the 1961 PGA Championship. Who is he?

69. Three non-American players were runners-up in the U.S. Open between 1972-1980. Who were they? Bonus: Two of them lost to the same man. Who was he?

70. Omnipresent at presentation ceremonies, who was Bobby Jones' friend and long-time Masters tournament director?

71. Who won the U.S. Open in 1901, 1903-1905?

72. Who won the second, third, fifth and eighth British Opens in 1861, 1862, 1864 and 1867?

73. The 1913 U.S. Open ended British domination of the game. Won by Francis Ouimet, it might have been won by Walter Hagen had Hagen not had an incredible start; what was it?

74. What was nicknamed the "Impregnable Quadrilateral"?

75. What year did the U.S.G.A. bring back the Open to The Country Club in Brookline, Massachusetts in honor of Francis Ouimet?

76. Who holds the record for number of times coming in second in the British Open? Bonus: How many, and in what years?

77. What was the first year since its inception the U.S. Open did not take place?

78. What tournaments did Bobby Jones win for his "Grand Slam" in 1930?

79. Who was the first amateur to win the U.S. Open?

80. What famous brothers both had a win in the PGA Championship (1950-1960)?

81. Name the 1984 Women's U.S. Open winner.

82. Sandra Haynie has won four LPGA Majors; which title has escaped her?

83. Tied for second in accumulated LPGA Majors are Betsy Rawls and Donna Caponi with how many each?

84. JoAnne Carner has won four majors. What are they?

85. How did Nicklaus win the 1962 Open?

86. What is the only Major Arnold Palmer has never won?

87. What courageous champion dropped his putter on the 18th at Congressional and said, "My God, I've won the Open"?

88. What amateur lost the 1956 Masters by only one stroke to pro Jackie Burke?

89. For years it was traditional that this man play the final round of the Masters with the leader. Who is he?

90. What was Sam Snead's first Major victory, and where was it played?

91. What Major escaped Sam Snead?

92. Who won the 1970 PGA at Southern Hills in Tulsa, Oklahoma?

93. How many times did Harry Vardon win the British Open?

94. The playoff for the 1947 Open involved what two PGA greats?

95. To win the 1932 U.S. Open, he played the last 28 holes in only 100 strokes. Who is he?

96. Who won the 1970 U.S. Open?

97. This father and son combo won eight of the first 12 British Opens. Who are they?

98. Name the site of the 1984 British Open. Bonus: Where was it *first* played, and in what year?

99. Who played in the most consecutive Opens — 27 between 1920 and 1950 (but none from 1942 to 1945)?

100. Name five of the sites where the British Open has been played since 1860.

101. The first twelve British Opens were played at the same course; which one?

102. Name the four Majors that comprise the modern "Grand Slam."

103. Who won the first Masters in 1934 with a score of 284?

104. How many times was Sam Snead runner-up in the U.S. Open?

105. Who was the first man to win four U.S. Opens?

106. Who won a Purple Heart for his efforts during the Battle of the Bulge, and

followed it up with a win at the 1946 U.S. Open?

107. Who won the U.S. Open on the Golden Anniversary of Ouimet's win?

108. Who won the second U.S. Open Championship?

109. Ben Hogan hit his historic 2-iron shot 200 yards against the wind on the 18th at what course to set up the playoff for the 1950 Open? Bonus: Who did Hogan end up beating?

110. What happened to Ben Hogan's famous 2-iron?

111. What second-year touring pro used his sister as his caddy in the 1984 Masters?

112. Which LPGA star has won the most Majors? Bonus: How many?

113. Who was the first professional to use a woman caddy at the Masters?

114. He averaged only three months a year of competitive play, yet achieved 13 Major victories over a seven-year period. Who was he?

For the following pros, give the number of professional Majors each has won, and name them for a bonus:

115. Jack Nicklaus

116. Tom Watson

117. Lee Trevino

118. Gary Player

119. Ben Hogan

120. Walter Hagen

121. Sam Snead

122. Gene Sarazen

123. Arnold Palmer

124. What kept Bobby Jones away from golf?

For the following questions, answer true or false:

125. Lee Trevino refuses to play at Augusta National in the Masters.

126. Ed "Porky" Oliver never won a Major.

127. Denny Shute won the U.S. PGA back-to-back.

128. Ben Hogan leads all with five U.S. Open titles.

129. Nancy Lopez-Knight has never won the U.S. Women's Open.

130. Sam Snead has finished second in the Masters three times.

131. Seve Ballesteros is the only Spaniard ever to win a Major.

132. Arnold Palmer has finished second in the U.S. Open five times.

133. Jack Nicklaus has finished second in the U.S. Open five times.

134. No amateur has ever won the Masters.

135. Gary Player is the only South African to win a Major.

136. Tony Jacklin is the only United Kingdom native to win the U.S. Open.

137. Jan Stephenson is the only Australian to win an LPGA Major.

138. Whose first professional win was the 1985 U.S. Women's Open at Baltusrol?

139. Who was the last British citizen to win the British Open prior to Sandy Lyle's 1985 victory at the Royal St. George's Golf Club in Sandwich?

140. What other major besides the 1985 U.S. PGA has Hubert Green won?

141. Other than his two U.S. Open wins in 1978 and 1985, has Andy North won any other majors?

# THE MEDIA

1. Who wrote *Confessions of a Hooker*?

2. Who wrote: "...riding with the Honorable Mayor and Horton Smith, our president of the PGA, through the narrow, majestic canyons of concrete and steel as the thousands cheered block after block — the confetti of paper tape ribbons which darkened the sky — certainly gave me a thrill which I've never experienced before."

3. Who is editor-in-chief of *Golf World*?

4. What ABC-TV golfcaster is a former British Ryder Cup player?

5. Jimmy Demaret was congratulating Chandler Harper on the radio for winning the 1953 World Championship — what interrupted the broadcast?

6. Who wrote *The Bogey Man?*

7. Name the PGA pro whose golf book was entitled *My Game and Yours*?

8. What BBC commentator also wrote *The Long Green Fairway* and *Masters of Golf*?

9. In "The Honeymooners," what did Art Carney do when Jackie Gleason screamed at him to address the ball?

10. Who was the first pro to give a TV golf lesson?

11. Who was the *Sports Illustrated* "Sportsman of the Year" in 1971?

12. This golf writer for the *Boston Globe* was once editor of "News & Views" of Harvard sports. Name him.

13. Who is editor-in-chief of *Golf Digest*?

14. What is "the most powerfully graceful action in sports"?

15. When asked about his health in 1962, who said, "I am in the full bloom of decay"?

16. Who said: "Golf is a lot like sex. It's something you can enjoy all your life...and, if you remain an amateur, you get to pick your own playing partners"?

17. The book *Comeback* had whose name in the subtitle?

18. Who is the author of *The Golf Connection*?

19. Who are the authors of *Teed Off*?

Name the network that televises the following golfing events:

20. The Masters

21. Panasonic/Las Vegas Invitational

22. Nabisco/Dinah Shore

23. Western Open

24. Bob Hope Classic

25. U.S. Women's Open

26. U.S. Open, British Open and PGA

27. Who wrote *The Good Sense of Golf*?

28. In what Agatha Christie novel is the corpse found on a golf course?

29. Who was *Golf World's* 1985 "Golfer of the Year"?

30. What NBC telecaster said: "I...was recommended to an acupuncture specialist, a Dr. Gonzalez. I thought all the experts in that field were Chinese and asked if this guy used switchblades..."?

31. Who publishes *Tour,* the official publication of the PGA Tour?

32. Who co-authored golf books with Hogan, Sarazen and Nicklaus?

33. Who is the dean of instruction at *Golf Digest*'s instruction schools?

34. Who wrote *Golf to Music*?

35. Whose slogan was "Stop to smell the flowers"?

36. In what Nancy Drew novel does Nancy play a golf match?

37. Who wrote *The Natural Way to Better Golf*?

38. In what James Bond novel does 007 play a golf match?

39. Who wrote *Go For Broke*?

40. Who played the pro Tour as an amateur and later became a distinguished golf columnist and author?

41. Who was Bob Jones' newspaper sidekick and biographer?

42. What was the first major telecast of a golf tournament?

43. Who wrote *Golf in the Kingdom*?

44. Who wrote the first American golf book?

45. The 1951 movie *Follow the Sun* starred Glenn Ford as what famous golfer?

46. Who hit the actual golf shots used in *Follow the Sun*?

47. *Golf Digest*'s playing editors include Amy Alcott, JoAnne Carner, Al Geiberger, David Graham, Hale Irwin, Tom Kite, Patty Sheehan, Sam Snead, Hal Sutton and Tom Watson. Who is the chief of this famous group?

48. Who covered the 1985 Masters for *Sports Illustrated*?

49. *Golf* Magazine's playing editors include Seve Ballesteros, Bobby Clampett, Ben Crenshaw, Ray Floyd, Gary Hallberg, Juli Inkster, Peter Jacobsen, Johnny Miller, Greg Norman and Ken Venturi. Who is the director of this illustrious group?

50. This noted CBS commentator makes only one golf broadcasting appearance per year (at the Masters). Who is he?

51. What noted golf writer, member of eight British Ryder Cup teams, wrote among other best-sellers *Bedside Golf* and *More Bedside Golf*?

52. What network does Marlene Floyd provide commentary for?

53. Charlie Jones provides commentary for what network?

54. Ed Sneed, who almost won the Masters in 1979, currently provides golf commentary for what major TV network?

55. Herbert Warren Wind is famed for the quality of his golf writing. What popular non-golf magazine does he currently write for?

56. Who wrote *Golfer's Gold*?

57. What long-time CBS announcer at the Masters is now with ABC?

58. What former pro-football great is now the anchor for CBS's Masters broadcast team?

59. What knowledgeable British broadcaster graced the 16th hole at Augusta for many Masters?

60. What former PGA winner is a member of ABCs broadcast team?

61. Who wrote *This Life I've Led*?

62. What former NFL quarterback is part of the NBC golf team?

63. What is the title of Bobby Jones' autobiography?

64. Jan Stephenson caused a furor in 1981 with her photo in what popular golf magazine?

65. What 1959 PGA winner and current ABC-TV commentator was famous for his baseball-like grip on the PGA Tour?

66. This famous TV entertainer now hosts her own golf tournament. Who is she?

67. For what network does former PGA star Steve Melnyk broadcast?

68. What former PGA star later played a role in the "I Love Lucy" show?

69. Who played Mildred D. Zaharias in the TV movie about her life entitled "Babe"? Bonus: What ex-NFL star played her husband in the movie, and is her husband in reality?

70. Who co-starred with Jane Wyman in the 1942 film *Shoot Yourself Some Golf*?

71. What famous golfer hosted the TV show "Golf for Swingers"?

72. Who was the first golfer to write an instruction book?

73. Who is NBC's executive producer for its PGA Tour telecasts?

74. Who is currently the British member of the CBS broadcasting team who covers the 16th hole for the Masters?

75. Who won the 1934 British Open and authored the *Illustrated History of Golf*?

76. Who holds the all-time record for lowest score on "Shell's Wonderful World of Golf" with a 65?

77. Who was George Plimpton's pro partner in the Bing Crosby Pro-Am in *The Bogey Man*? Bonus: What was the first name of Plimpton's caddy?

78. What former PGA winner is a member of NBC's broadcast team?

79. Who wrote *The Education of a Woman Golfer*?

80. Who is the CBS executive producer/director famed for his Masters presentation?

81. Who wrote *The Hole Truth*?

82. Who usually joins Trevino in the broadcasting tower at the 18th?

83. Jay Randolph provides golf commentary for what major network?

84. Who wrote *Golf My Way*?

85. What former British Open Champion provides golf commentary for CBS?

86. Who wrote *The Story of American Golf*?

87. Twice runner-up at the Masters, what noted golfer now provides Masters commentary for CBS?

88. True or False: Jim Simpson, Jim Thacker, Roger Twibell, Nick Seitz and Lou Palmer all provide golf commentary for ESPN.

89. Mary Bea Porter and Mary Bryan currently provide golf commentary for which network?

90. What Australian — with eight U.S. Tour wins — has provided golf commentary for NBC and ESPN?

91. True or False: Verne Lunquist, Mark Carlson, Frank Guber, Bob Drum, Tom Roy and Bob Daily are all members of the CBS golf team.

92. What golf commentator for both CBS and the BBC became the fourth player to represent Great Britain in both Walker and Ryder Cup play when he was chosen for the 1973 Ryder Cup?

93. Does Jim McKay ever provide golf commentary for ABC?

94. What book by Ben Hogan, originally published in 1957, is still considered a classic of golf instruction?

95. In what major magazine was the preceding book originally serialized?

96. Who prepared the illustrations that helped to explain the text: (a) Anthony Ravielli, (b) Sidney L. James, (c) A.S. Barnes?

97. What noted golf broadcaster attempted to get a tour card for the 1986 PGA Senior Tour? Did he get his card?

98. True or False: Ohlmeyer Communications is producer of the Tour's senior events and the LPGA Tour.

99. Who was *Golf Digest's* 1985 World Player of the Year?

# THE PROS

1. Cary Middlecoff was trained for what profession?

2. Who won the 1985 Bing Crosby at Pebble Beach?

3. Who made up the foursome in the 1983 inaugural Skins Game, and who was the big winner?

4. Who is the "Walrus"?

5. Who made the longest string of consecutive cuts on the Tour?

6. Who shaved off 40 pounds in 1965 by eating buffalo meat, ground deer meat, and reindeer stew?

7. What resident of St. Simons Island, Georgia was once a back-up quarterback to Don Meredith?

8. Who is nicknamed "Fuzzy"?

9. Who holds the LPGA record for most consecutive Tour victories?

10. Who holds the record for the most money won on the PGA Tour in a single season?

11. His 59 in the 1977 Danny Thomas Memphis Classic is a PGA Tour record. Who is he?

12. Name the first player on the LPGA Tour to hail from South Africa.

13. The father of this LPGA Tour member is a teaching pro, and her brother is a top PGA player. Who is she?

14. What former Yankee pitcher from Larned, Kansas is now a PGA pro?

15. Name three Austrialian players active on the PGA Tour.

16. Who were the first two women elected to the World Golf Hall of Fame?

17. What controversial, outspoken Tour player filed a $3 million lawsuit in 1970 against the Tournament Players Division?

18. Who was the top money winner of the 1985 Tournament Players Series?

19. What is Gil Morgan's "other" profession?

20. Who was the winner of the 1985 PGA Assistant Professional Championship?

21. Who is known as "Big Momma"?

22. Name the two Canadians who teamed up to win the 1968 World Cup.

23. Name the British star — now on the PGA Tour — who won the 1974 French Open.

24. Who won every tournament he entered in 1953?

25. What was the highest 72-hole winning score on both the 1984 and 1985 LPGA Tour?

26. Who was the winner of the 1985 Seiko-Tucson Match Play Championship?

27. PGA Tour members Jerry Pate and Bruce Lietzke are brothers-in-law. What are their wives' names?

28. How much did Paul Runyan earn as top money winner in 1934?

29. Name two famous "wiffs."

30. Who was the 1985 PGA club pro Player of the Year?

31. She rides a motorcycle and qualified for the LPGA Hall of Fame by winning the Women's World Championship in 1982. Who is she?

32. Who holds the record for consecutive tournament victories? Bonus: How many?

33. Who is considered to be the man who brought golf pros "out of the club room" to their present status?

34. Who is considered the first "professional" golfer?

35. What was the occasion of the longest sudden-death playoff? Bonus: Who won?

36. Who is called "The Spaceman"?

37. What pro carried on a simultaneous career as a pop singer?

38. Who was "Titanic Thompson"?

39. What was Jack Nicklaus' first pro victory?

40. This modern great earned $80 a month as an orderly in a psychiatric clinic before entering the world of pro golf. Who is he?

41. Who was famous for his late-tournament "charges"?

42. With over $3 million, he is the #3 all-time moneymaker. His first year on the Tour (1966), he made $600. Who is he?

43. Who was nicknamed the "Bantam"?

44. Who is nicknamed "Super Mex"?

45. This diminutive Massachusetts native is acknowledged to be one of the game's finest teachers. Who is he?

46. Name the pro who is a direct descendant from the signer of the Declaration of Independence from New Jersey.

47. Arnold Palmer's father was also a golf pro. What was his first name?

48. What Tour player is the son of a famous character actor?

49. Who sunk the longest putt of his professional career at the Desert Inn Country Club during the Tournament of Champions in 1953-1966: Sam Snead, Art Wall, Jack Nicklaus, or Billy Casper?

50. What was the top purse on the 1985 LPGA Tour?

51. Who was the "Slammer"?

52. Who is the top player from 1954 to 1968 recently inducted into the Carolinas' Golf Hall of Fame?

53. The 1962 L.A. Open was Jack Nicklaus' maiden Tour event. How did he fare?

54. Who won the Crosby and Hawaiian Opens back-to-back in 1985?

55. Who was the winner of the 1985 Rhode Island Open?

56. Who won the 1985 Colorado Open?

57. This PGA great now hosts a juniors golf camp in La Jolla, California. Who is he?

58. Who is "Dr. Dirt"?

59. Who was the captain of the 1983 U.S. Ryder Cup Team?

60. Who is "the other Watson"?

61. Who was unanimously selected captain of the 1985 U.S. Ryder Cup Team?

62. Who invented the sand wedge?

63. Who won the first Tournament of Champions held at the Desert Inn Country Club in 1953, and what was the prize?

64. Who played on both the U.S. pro tennis circuit and the PGA Tour?

65. Who is the touring pro at the Doral Hotel and Country Club?

66. Who led the Asian Order of Merit in 1984?

67. Who is nicknamed "Sandy"?

68. Who set a new tournament record at the TPC in 1985?

69. What collegiate All-American from Wake Forest has Masters champ Bob Goalby for his uncle and mentor?

70. What resident of Chattanooga, Tennessee is remembered at Pinehurst for a record 62 during the World Open?

71. Who is called "Mighty Mite"?

72. Who has an incredible string of 117

cuts made?

73. Who was 1985 Men's Rookie of the Year?

74. Why was 1984 Pat Bradley's "bridesmaid year"?

75. Who is nicknamed "Babe"?

76. Name six pairs of pro golfing brothers.

77. Who is Dorado Beach's touring pro?

78. Who is the youngest player on the PGA Tour in 1986?

79. Known as "Mr. Straight," his tee shots in 1983 hit the fairway with an incredible 85% consistency. Who is he?

80. Name the 1960s "Athlete of the Decade."

81. Who is nicknamed "Doc"?

82. What is J.C. Snead's relationship to Sam Snead?

83. He holds nine of the 18 course records on Hilton Head Island. Who is he?

84. Despite not living up to his predicted potential, he is #8 on the all-time money list. Who his he?

85. Who is "Little Poison"?

86. Full of heart, this 1965 U.S. Amateur champ and 1968 Rookie of the Year

was born on Valentines Day in 1945. Who is he?

87. Who had the best (70.70) before-the-cut scoring average in 1984?

88. What did Bruce Lietzke, Jack Nicklaus, Greg Norman and Tom Watson share in 1984?

89. Who is "Wild Bill"?

90. Name the four founders of the LPGA in 1950.

91. Who was named one of America's ten best dressed jocks in 1973 and one of the "Ten Sexiest Athletes in America" by *Pageant*?

92. Who is nicknamed "Jug"?

93. Who is the LPGA's first $100,000-in-a-season winner?

94. She was a teenage caddy in Maine and her list of victories includes the 1975 U.S. Women's Open. Who is she?

95. Who was nicknamed "Champagne Tony"?

96. He won the 1960 Crosby in some of the worst weather ever, even though he shot 77 on the final day. Who is he?

97. What former U.S. Tennis Open and Wimbledon winner also played on the LPGA Tour?

98.  What LPGA star is married to a major league baseball player?

99.  What talented husband-and-wife team is active on the LPGA and PGA Tours?

100. Who is called "The Machine"?

101. Whose theme is "swing easy, hit hard"?

102. Whose 257 for 72 holes in the 1955 Texas Open is still a PGA record?

103. Who was the 1983 PGA and TPC winner named Player of the Year?

104. Who is "The Chief"?

105. Who holds the all-time record for Tour victories?

106. Who holds the PGA record for most tournament wins?

107. Which two players hold the record for most consecutive birdies on a PGA Tour?

108. Who is "The Hawk"?

109. Who was the man who taught Jack Nicklaus how to play?

110. Who was the youngest female touring pro ever? (She is still on tour.)

111. Who is nicknamed "Light Horse" Harry?

112. Born in 1914, he was known as the

"Candy Kid" on the Tour. Who is he?

113. This former outfielder for the New York Yankees won two PGA crowns in 1945. Who is he?

114. Who stopped Nelson's winning streak at 11 in 1945?

115. The 1983 Player of the Year won the PGA Championship at Riviera. Who is he?

116. Who won the 1985 Los Angeles Open by seven strokes?

117. Who was the top winner in the 1984 Skins Game?

118. Who started the 1985 PGA Tour season by playing 109 holes without a bogie?

119. Who won the 1985 Hope Desert Classic? Bonus: Whom did he beat in the five-hole playoff?

120. Who is "The Silver Scot"?

121. He won the first pro tournament he played in, the 1956 Byron Nelson Classic. Who is he?

122. Who won the first Byron Nelson Classic in 1944?

123. How many times has Sam Snead won the Greater Greensboro Open?

124. With what Fort Worth tournament

was Ben Hogan associated?

125. Name the American Indian high on the money list for three different years.

126. Who is the all-time winningest player, with 241 official tournament victories?

127. Who won the 1985 Tournament of Champions?

128. What golfer was first to crack the $1 million mark in career earnings?

129. Who joined the pro golf circuit after a successful pro hockey career?

130. Who shot the lowest nine-hole score on the 1985 LPGA Tour?

131. Who is known as "Mr. X"?

132. Known for playing it safe, he is "safely" on the all-time money list in the #6 slot. Who is he?

133. Who is the only Alaskan on tour?

134. This Hall of Famer ranks #16 on the all-time money list — luckily, because he has 11 children. Who is he?

135. What is Lee Trevino's middle name?

136. What Alabama-born, 1983 Open winner gives credit to being "born again"?

137. This native of Worcester, Massachu-

setts won the L.A. Open back-to-back in 1954 and 1955. Who is he?

138. From Bindura, Zimbabwe, he is making a mark on the Tour. Who is he?

139. Shirley Spork, 1983 LPGA Teacher of the Year, was #10 on the money list in 1950. How much did she earn?

140. Name the famous LPGA golf ambassador from Hawaii.

141. Who joined the pro Tour in 1965 after attending Kansas State on a football scholarship?

142. This links artist, who won nearly $250,000 in 1984, taught himself how to play. Who is he?

143. These two skilled golfers are in great demand for exhibitions and clinics as a comedy team which imitates other players. Name them.

144. This Edmond, Oklahoma star is considered to have a nearly flawless swing. Who is he?

145. This 6'2" Brigham Young grad was the 1973 Open champ, the 1974 PGA Player of the Year, and the 1976 British Open Champ. He pulled in over $139,000 on the Tour in 1984 after a slump. Who is he?

146. What pro holds the unofficial record for the most courses played in a lifetime?

147. Who is the only person to win the PGA Long Drive Championship twice?

148. What was Ed Oliver's nickname?

149. Who were the American and British captains of the first Ryder Cup match?

150. Who is "The Moose"?

151. What was Jack Nicklaus' profession before he turned pro?

152. What PGA golfer holds the record for holes-in-one?

153. Who was 1984 LPGA leading money winner?

154. What team beat Miller Barber and Julius Boros in the 1984 "Legends of Golf" tourney?

155. As of January 1, 1986, who is the all-time leading money winner?

156. Who was the leading money winner on the Senior Tour in 1985?

157. What world-famous golfer is a native of Buenos Aires?

158. Who was the "human siege gun"?

159. Craig Stadler held what PGA stats record in both 1984 and 1985?

160. Who had the best PGA putts-per-round average with 28.627 in 1985?

161. Who led the 1985 Tour in driving,

with a 278.2 yard average?

162. Who holds the 1985 scoring average Vardon Trophy?

163. Who won the 1985 Bob Jones Award for sportsmanship?

164. The "Gilroy Cowboy" is one of the best putters of all time. Who is he?

165. Who was the top European player awarded the 1985 Order of Merit?

166. Who is the "Thunderbolt"?

167. Who led the 1985 Tour in eagles?

168. Who was the 1985 PGA Tour Player of the Year?

169. Who is the "Great White Shark"?

170. Who led the 1985 PGA Tour in total birdies?

171. Who holds the LPGA record with 88 tournament victories?

172. Who led the 1985 LPGA Tour in scoring?

173. Who is Eugene Saraceni?

174. What was Paul Harney's first pro victory?

175. What record did Bob Goalby set while winning the St. Petersburg Open?

176. Who blamed his bad shots on his

clubs, and dragged the offenders down the highway behind his car to "punish" them?

177. Who is the "Golden Bear"?

178. Who won the Ben Hogan Award in 1984?

179. What is Lee Trevino's logo?

180. Who brandishes and sheaths his putter like a sword after sinking a crucial putt?

181. He won nine tournaments his rookie year on tour. Who is he?

182. Whose trademark is the trouser-hitch?

183. What deliberate player combed his hair before almost every shot, infuriating his opponents?

184. Who was "Lord Byron"?

185. Who were the "gold-dust twins"?

186. Whom did the Scots call the "Wee Ice Mon"?

187. To whom did Queen Elizabeth present the OBE (Officer of the British Empire) on her birthday in 1970?

188. Name the world's most successful left-handed golfer.

189. Who were "The Big Three"?

190. What two players were nicknamed "Sarge"?

191. What brother-sister team was the winner of the 1985 J.C. Penney Mixed Team Classic?

192. Who was the first Canadian to win a U.S. Tour event?

193. Name the top teaching professional who conducts comprehensive two and three day golf workshops at the famed Doral in Miami.

194. His nickname is Papwa, and he won the Dutch Open in 1959, 1960 and 1964. Who is he? Bonus: What was unusual about his grip?

195. What was Ben Hogan's greatest year?

196. Name the tournaments Ben Hogan won in his greatest year.

197. Which of these foreign members of the PGA Tour won a tour event in 1985: Dennis Watson, Greg Norman, Nick Faldo or Seve Ballesteros?

198. Who is "Dutch"?

199. What is Chi Chi Rodriguez' real name?

200. What was golf's first $50,000 first prize? Bonus: Who won?

201. Where was the tournament with golf's first $50,000 first prize held?

202. Who had the highest percentage of greens hit in regulation on the 1985 PGA Tour?

203. What player had the biggest winning margin in 1985?

204. Match the partners of the 1985 J.C. Penney Mixed Team Classic:

    a) Craig Stadler        1. Patty Sheehan
    b) Curtis Strange       2. Beth Daniel
    c) Al Geiberger         3. Vicki Alvarez
    d) William Kratzert     4. Jane Geddes
    e) Tom Kite             5. Joanne Carner
    f) Mike Donald          6. Lori Garbacz
    g) John Mahaffey        7. Nancy Lopez
    h) Larry Mize           8. Cathy Kratzert
    i) Jim Thorpe           9. Martha Nause

205. What does the winner of the Sea Pines Heritage Classic receive besides a trophy and prize money?

206. Who is Spain's only representative on the LPGA Tour?

207. Match the golfer with his 1985 title:

    1. Bob Hope Classic      (a) Curtis Strange
    2. Bing Crosby           (b) Mark McCumber
       Pro-Am                (c) Mark O'Meara
    3. Doral-Eastern Open    (d) Tom Kite
    4. MONY-Tournament       (e) Lanny Wadkins
       of Champions
    5. Panasonic-Las
       Vegas International

208. This Tour star was a former co-captain of the University of Colorado football team. Who is he?

209. Who was the president of the PGA of America for 1985?

210. Ben Hogan served in the U.S. Armed Services during WWII. What was his

branch of service?

211.   What tournament had the largest purse of all the events on the 1985 PGA Tour?

212.   Who has won more championships in golf—Nicklaus or Palmer?

213.   What year did Jack Nicklaus win his first national tournament?

214.   In 1982, Jerry Pate celebrated his victory at the TPC by taking a dip in the lake bordering the 18th green. What two VIPs did he take with him into the lake?

215.   On what occasion had Pate previously celebrated a victory by jumping in a lake?

216.   What was considered to Sam Snead's biggest weakness on the golf course?

217.   What PGA Tour member plays righthanded but putts lefthanded?

218.   Who was the first South African to enter the world of golf in America and win over $20,000 in prize money in 1947?

219.   Who was to become the most popular new golfer after Ben Hogan?

220.   What year did Arnold Palmer win his first PGA Tour competition?

221. Match the golfer with her 1985 LPGA title:

    1. DuMaurier Classic        (a) Joanne Carner
    2. Safeco Classic           (b) Alice Miller
    3. Nabisco Dinah Shore       (c) Pat Bradley
       Invitational             (d) Patty Sheehan
    4. Sarasota Classic

222. The professional world record for career holes-in-one is 45. Known as "The King of Aces," this professional also owns the record for double eagles with a total of 10. Who is he?

223. What professional golfer holds the all-time lowest Vardon Trophy Honor?

224. What famous golfer went into retirement in 1930 and made it a rule to make only one appearance per year in competition?

225. What was the last year prior to 1985 that the U.S. Pro's lost the Ryder Cup?

# THE AMATEURS

1. How old was Bobby Jones when he won the Georgia State Amateur?

2. Marie Robie of Wollaston, Massachusetts holds the women's record for length of a hole-in-one. How long was it?

3. What tourney did Jose-Maria Olazabal win in 1984?

4. Who was the U.S.G.A. president when the first Walker Cup was played?

5. Name the two Curtis sisters for whom the Curtis Cup is named?

6. Who was the "Emperor of Golf"?

7. What distinguished milestone does the British Amateur celebrate in 1985?

8. Who won the NCAA Team Championship more times than any other college?

9. Who won the 1984 U.S. Amateur?

True or False: Each of the following has won the U.S. Amateur. (If the answer is "true," give the year he/she won.)

10. Pat Bradley

11. Nancy Lopez

12. Beth Daniel

13. Jane Blalock

14. Louise Suggs

15. Patty Berg

16. Jackie Pung

17. Catherine Lacoste

18. Started in 1878, it is the oldest amateur golf competition in the world. What is it?

19. Who won the British Amateur Championship in three consecutive years (1968-1970)?

20. Who won the U.S. Amateur in three consecutive years (1980-1982)?

21. Who was the first amateur to win the Canadian Open?

22. Who was the six-time winner of the U.S. Ladies Amateur between 1922-1935?

23. Name the colleges attended by Jack Nicklaus, Arnold Palmer and Tom Watson.

24. Who was the first U.S. citizen to win the British Amateur Championship?

25. Who was the only Briton to win the U.S. Amateur?

26. Who defeated Bob Jones in the finals of the 1926 U.S. Amateur?

What college/school did the following players attend?

27. Bob Goalby

28. Juli Inkster

29. Nancy Lopez

30. Andy Bean

31. Ben Crenshaw

32. Bobby Clampett

33. John Cook

34. Peter Jacobsen

35. Gil Morgan

36. Mike Nicolette

37. Jerry Pate

38. Corey Pavin

39. Craig Stadler

40. Hal Sutton

41. Willie Wood

42. Fuzzy Zoeller

43. Billy Casper

44. Paul Harney

45. Don January

46. Orville Moody

47. Jan Stephenson

48. Who captured both the U.S. and British Amateur back-to-back in 1934 and 1935?

49. Who were the 1985 NCAA Division I team champions?

50. Name three amateurs who have won the U.S. Open.

51. Who was the last amateur to win the U.S. Open?

52. What golfer won the NCAA championship three years running?

53. How many amateurs have won the U.S. Open?

54. Who won the 1985 Mid-Amateur?

55. How many times did Chick Evans win the Western Amateur?

56. Who started playing golf at age 35 and won three U.S. Amateurs and the British Amateur, among others?

57. When was the first Walker Cup played?

58. Name the 1984 California Amateur Champion who played for UCLA.

59. Who won the 1947 Ladies Amateur Championship?

True or False: Each of the following has won the NCAA. (If the answer is "true," give the year he/she won.)

60. Bob Jones

61. Hale Irwin

62. Nathaniel Crosby

63. John Mahaffey

64. Jack Nicklaus

65. Tom Watson

66. Ben Crenshaw

67. Tom Kite

68. Jess Sweetser

69. Francis Ouimet

70. Arnold Palmer

71.  Kermit Zarley

72.  Tom Weiskopf

73.  Kathy Whitworth

74.  Juli Inkster

75.  Hollis Stacy

76.  Cindy Hill

77.  Nancy Lopez

78.  Who, as an amateur, lost the 1956 Masters by one stroke?

79.  Who won five U.S. Women's Amateurs?

80.  Who was the 1982 U.S. Open Women's Champ?

81.  What is the amateur record for most courses played in a lifetime?

82.  Who won the 1959 U.S. Amateur?

83.  Brooklyn-born, he attended the University of Florida on a basketball scholarship. His rookie year on tour, he tied for second in the Westchester Classic and later won two others. Who is he?

84.  Where was the first U.S. Amateur Championship held?

85.  Name the first year Britain won the Walker Cup.

86. Which country won the Curtis Cup from 1932 to 1950?

87. What do amateurs Jeff Long, John Mc-Cormick and Andy Franks have in common?

88. Name the award that is considered college golf's equivalent of the Heisman Trophy.

89. Who was the winner of the 1985 U.S.G.A. Girls' Junior?

90. Who was the winner of the 1985 U.S.G.A. Boys' Junior?

91. What was the name of the 1935 Massachusetts Amateur Champion who invented the Stimpmeter?

92. How old was Bobby Jones when he retired from competitive golf?

93. Who was the winner of the Women's 1985 Public Links and NCAA's?

94. Called the "Bobby Jones of women's golf," she was the greatest woman golfer of the 1920s. Who was she, and how many titles did she win during her career?

95. What golfer won three consecutive Women's Amateur titles in 1932-1934?

For the following questions, answer true or false:

96. New England's Ted Bishop won the U.S. Amateur.

97. New England's Julius Boros won the U.S. Amateur.

98. Bing Crosby once competed in the U.S. Amateur.

99. Nathaniel Crosby won the U.S. Amateur at Pebble Beach.

100. Attorney Vinny Giles won the U.S. Amateur.

101. PGA Tour Director Deane Beman won the U.S. Amateur.

102. Ben Crenshaw won the U.S. Amateur.

103. Tom Kite won the U.S. Amateur.

104. Membership in New England's "Par Club" is limited to golfers who have matched par for a round.

105. Born in Victoria, Australia, he won the U.S. Amateur in 1900 in his fourth year of golf. Who is he?

106. Who won the U.S. Amateur in 1907 and 1908?

107. Who succeeded Babe Zaharias as U.S. Amateur and British Amateur Champion in 1947 and 1948?

108. Who did Arnold Palmer defeat in the 1954 U.S. Amateur final?

109. Born in 1955, she won the U.S. Ladies Amateur in 1971 to become the

youngest winner since 1896. Who is she?

110. Who won both the British and the U.S. Amateurs in 1967?

111. True or False: Angela Bonallack, the wife of former British Walker Cup Captain Michael Bonallack, played on the British Curtis Cup team.

112. When did the British side last win the Walker Cup?

113. What amateur won a PGA Tour event in 1985? What event did he win?

114. This junior girl won the 1985 U.S. Women's Amateur. Who is she?

115. Who was the winner of the 1985 U.S.G.A. Senior Amateur Championship?

# THE EQUIPMENT

1. True or False: A "two-piece" ball has a solid core.

2. What are the two most popular covers of the golf ball?

3. Who invented the modern golf ball (rubber center)?

4. What is a "leather mashie"?

5. What is a "hand mashie"?

6. Name the year the PGA reduced the number of clubs one could carry from 16 to 14.

7. What is a "feathery"?

8. What number was usually found on old putters?

9. What are "baffies" and "jiggers"?

For the following modern terms, give the out-moded names:

10. 2-Wood

11. 3-Wood

12. 4-Wood

13. 1-Iron

14. 2-Iron

15. 3-Iron

16. 5-Iron

17. 6-Iron

18. 7-Iron

19. 8-Iron

20. 9-Iron

21. What was a common cure for a loose club head on wooden shafted irons?

22. From what wood were the shafts of old golf clubs made?

23. What immortal player sometimes carried up to four putters in his bag due to his erratic putting?

24. What sportswear has the alligator logo?

25. What are "plus-fours"?

26. Who invented the ping putter?

27.  What club did Alan Shephard hit on the surface of the moon?

28.  Who won the 1965 U.S. Open with fiberglass shafts?

29.  Where is the hosel located?

30.  For whom does Ray Floyd advertise on his golf bag?

31.  What is the standard loft on a driver?

32.  Before wooden pegs, what was used to elevate the ball for driving?

33.  Who was the winner of the 1984 Long Driving Contest? Bonus: What was unusual about his win?

34.  What is a "gutty"?

35.  What unusual equipment helped Walter J. Travis win the 1901 U.S. Amateur at the Atlantic City Country Club?

36.  What tour great used women's clubs his first 2½ years in the pros?

37.  Miller designed them, Norman nails them and Stadler swears by them; what are they?

38.  Dave Pelz manufactures what in Abilene?

39.  What clubs were played by Larry Nelson in winning the 1984 Walt Disney World Classic?

Name the club or club manufacturer represented by the following players:

40. Calvin Peete

41. Gary Player

42. Fuzzy Zoeller

43. Lanny Wadkins

44. Hollis Stacy

45. Arnold Palmer

46. Tom Kite, Hale Irwin and Jerry Pate, among others.

47. Tom Watson

48. Tom Weiskopf and Judy Rankin

49. What type of cover is on the Titleist Low Trajectory 100 golf ball, surlyn or balata?

50. What company's pro line is called "Ultras"?

51. Who manufactures Titleist golf balls?

52. Who manufactures Pro Staff golf balls?

53. What is the most popular golf ball on the PGA tour?

54. Jack Nicklaus plays with what line of clubs and balls?

55. True or False: Graphite shafts are heavier than regular steel shafts.

56. What company introduced the metal-wood club?

57. Who manufactures XL Top-Flite balls?

58. What are the classic golf shoes worn by most PGA & LPGA pros?

59. Who or what is "Calamity Jane"?

60. Before the advent of boxes or pails on the teeing ground, from where did the golfers obtain their sand?

61. How many clubs did Chick Evans use in winning both the U.S. Open and the U.S. Amateur in 1916? Bonus: Name the clubs.

62. What type of ball replaced the "feathery"?

63. Tom Watson promotes what well-known investment company?

64. What major automobile company helps sponsor the Masters telecasts?

65. What golf club manufacturer features "Roberto de Vicenzo Qualifier-Lites"?

66. What well-known moving company is the official sponsor of the National PGA Junior Championship?

67. How many dimples did the 1985 Top-Flight Plus have?

68. What golf club manufacturer produces a line of clubs under the brand name of "Fireball"?

69. What is the Stimpmeter?

70. How many dimples did the 1985 Wilson Staff golf ball have?

71. John Jacobs advertises golf clubs for what British company?

72. For what watch company does Arnold Palmer advertise?

73. What club manufacturer, famous for its metal woods, co-sponsored the 1985 PGA Match Play Championship?

74. Who sponsored the 1985 PGA Stroke Play Championship?

75. What manufacturer advertises itself as "America's first clubmaker"?

76. What golf ball manufacturer boasts that its ball has conquered the Grand Canyon?

77. Who or what is "Iron Byron"?

78. What golf shoe company is currently known as "Tom Watson's Choice"?

79. What golf shoe does Jack Nicklaus endorse?

80. True or False: Mizuno Golf Company is based in Japan.

# TRIVIAL TRIVIA

1. What is Ben Hogan's hometown?

2. Who is the commissioner of the LPGA?

3. This player, agent, golfer, and attorney represents Arnold Palmer, among others. Who is he?

4. Who was the first PGA tournament director?

5. Who is said to be the world's best putter?

6. Who is Nathaniel "Ironman" Avery?

7. Who was Arnold Palmer's regular caddy during his most successful year on the tour?

8. Who is Deane Beman?

9. Who was the first T.P.D. Commissioner?

10. In what year did the LPGA institute the qualifying school?

11. What PGA Tour star's wife is a former Miss Minnesota?

12. Who was elected for a second term as president of the U.S.G.A. in 1985?

13. What is the record for holes-in-one in a single round and who holds it?

14. Who holds the record in the National Long Driving Championship?

15. What is the longest drive ever hit during competitive play?

16. Who hit the longest drive in major competition?

17. Who was Samuel Ryder?

18. What is Jack Nicklaus' wife's name?

19. What is Bobby Jones' full name?

20. For what is the Horton Smith Award given?

21. Who was the Massachusetts Junior Champion in 1919 and 1920 who caddied for Francis Ouimet in the 1913 Open?

22. Before becoming tournament director for the PGA, who was at one time an FBI agent?

23. What was Ben Hogan's first wife's name?

24. Who is thought to be the "inventor" of the PGA Tour?

25. Who was the owner and operator of the Tam O'Shanter during the 1950s?

26. He holds the world record for career holes-in-one. Who is he?

27. In 1977 at Shady Oaks Country Club in Fort Worth, Texas, what did Ben Hogan do?

28. What is the name of Willie Wood's wife?

29. What pro trick-shot artist played boxer Joe Palooka in the movies?

30. Which golfing president did galleries fear the most?

31. Who installed a putting green outside the Oval Office?

32. Are pros allowed to wear Bermuda shorts on the tour?

33. What presidential golfer weighed over 300 pounds?

34. What was the nickname given to Bernhard Langer by *Sports Illustrated* after he won the Masters?

35. Why was 1912 an important year to the future of U.S. golf?

36. There is a mower mark in your line of putt. Are you allowed to fix it?

37. What year was the U.S.G.A. Publinx first played?

38. Who sponsored the first National Scrambler Championship (1984)?

39. What does GIR stand for?

40. What British monarch was elected captain of the Royal and Ancient in 1922?

41. What style of putting was outlawed at the 1895 U.S. Amateur in Newport, Rhode Island? Bonus: Who won the tournament?

42. What is the name of the PGA of America's championship award?

43. What's a "gimme"?

44. What is a "shotgun start"?

45. What is a "Miami Scramble"?

46. What year was the U.S. PGA organized?

47. What was the original title of the Vardon Trophy?

48. At what age is a PGA pro eligible for the "Senior" Tour?

49. In Massachusetts, it's the Ouimet; in Illinois, the Chick Evans; and in Rhode Island, the John Burke. What is it?

50. What are the "blue tees"?

51. Do men or women have the highest possible handicap for 18 holes?

52. What is the previous name of the World Cup competition?

53. What is a "greenie"?

54. What was the first year in which the Canadian Open was played?

55. Why are players from the pre-television era considered "iron men"?

56. What is a golf starter?

57. What is *Jeu de Mail*?

58. What were "rabbits"?

59. What unusual event marked the 1975 Western Open?

60. What is the term used for a deuce on a par 5?

61. Whom was the overlapping grip named after?

62. What year was the stymie abolished?

63. In 1985, the prize money for the Western Open was $500,000. What was the total prize money the first year the Open was played?

64. Before motorization, how did golf courses trim their acres of fairways?

65. What is a score of 5 on a par 3 hole called?

66. What is the difference between match and medal play?

67. What is the U.S.G.A. yardage guideline for a par 6?

68. How much money did the PGA Tour donate to charity in 1985?

69. What is an eagle on a par 3?

70. What scandal was dubbed "The Silver Spoons Classic"?

71. Jack Nicklaus hosts the Memorial Tournament at Muirfield Village. What year was the first Memorial held?

72. How many children do Jack and Barbara Nicklaus have? Bonus: Name them.

73. What are the odds against a hole-in-one?

74. What is the LPGA version of the Vardon trophy?

75. What beer magnate started his own country club when he was "socially unacceptable" at the existing St. Louis club?

76. On what basis is the Vardon Trophy awarded?

77. What French word did the term "caddy" derive from? Bonus: What does it mean?

78. Who was the first American captain of the Royal and Ancient Golf Club?

79. The granddaughter of James IV, while being educated in France, was the first to employ *cadets.* Who was she?

80. What was Arnold Palmer's most unusual drive in 1976?

81. What do the initials "ITL" stand for?

82. Who is the only man ever to hold an honorary membership on the PGA Tour?

83. Tony Jacklin once tried to hit a golf ball across the Thames. Did he make it?

84. Who was the 1985 recipient of the Donald Ross Award of the American Society of Golf Course Architects?

85. How many public golf courses are currently in West Germany?

86.  What is a shank?

87.  Where did the term "birdie" originate?

88.  Who originated the term, "Never up, never in," and to what stroke does it refer?

89.  What are the so-called "short" golf balls used at the new Grand Cayman Nicklaus course?

90.  What is known as Scotch golf?

91.  What is the most common 18-hole par around the world?

92.  What is the "perfect" distribution of holes?

Identify the following logos:

93.

94.

95.

96.

97.

98. How many people in the U.S. play at least a couple of rounds of golf a year?

99. What is the name of the first American golf club?

100. Who is the "Father of American Golf," who established the first American golf club in the U.S.?

101. Which *two* countries lay claim to initiating the game of golf?

102. Which country has been generally accepted as the originator of golf as we know it today?

103. Name the first golf club established in North America.

69

104. Where was the first American club-house built?

105. Who played the first game of golf in a public park?

106. Who was the first American to gain renown as a long hitter?

107. This member of ice hockey's Hall of Fame won the NHL scoring title and played on an NHL Stanley Cup Championship team in the 1920s; later he coached a Stanley Cup Championship team and served as Harvard College's hockey and golf coach in the 1950s and 1960s. Who is he?

108. Who was "The Great Young Man" of golf?

109. Who is known as "The Great Old Man" of golf?

110. Name three competitions the British and the Americans engage in each year.

111. Name the Boston Red Sox star who turned to pro golf, but did not qualify for the Tour?

112. What is the Richardson Award?

113. What is the Joe Graffis Award?

114. Who won the Joe Graffis Award for 1984?

115. What two famous tour events are played over five rounds instead of the standard four?

116. True or False: Bob Jones received a varsity "H" from Harvard University.

117. True or False: Bernhard Langer is a native of Germany.

118. True or False: Sally Little is a native of South Africa.

119. Did Arnold Palmer, the general of "Arnie's Army," ever serve in the military?

120. Whose outfit is invariably black? Bonus: Why?

121. What city has "more golf per square foot" than any other place in the world?

122. What was the name of the hurricane that almost caused the 1985 PGA Assistants Championship to be cancelled?

# THE COURSES

1. Name the golf resort where the movie *Caddyshack* was filmed.

2. Where was the first Ryder Cup match played?

3. Where was the 1985 U.S.G.A. Women's Amateur played?

4. Located 12 miles from Charleston on the Isle of Palms is a new resort golf course designed by Tom Fazio. Name it.

5. Name the three golf courses that guests at Sea Pines Plantation on Hilton Head Island have to conquer.

6. The "Teeth of the Dog" and "The Links," both designed by Pete Dye, are located at what resort in the Caribbean?

7. The Doral Hotel & Country Club is famous for "The Blue Monster." What are the names of its other four courses?

8. What resort, host of the Tournament of Champions, has for its last three holes "the longest mile in golf"?

9. What was the scene of Bobby Locke's first British Open win in 1949?

Name the site that hosts each of the following tournaments:

10. Merrill Lynch/Golf Digest Commemorative Pro-Am

11. Bank of Boston Classic

12. Kemper Open

13. Sea Pines Heritage Classic

14. Boston Five Classic

15. Nabisco/Dinah Shore Invitational

16. MONY Tournament of Champions

17. Tournament Players Championship

18. The PGA Seniors

19. Western Open

20. NBC World Series of Golf

21. North & South Championship

22. 1988 U.S. Open

23. 1985 U.S. Open

24. 1985 LPGA Championship

25.  1984 U.S. Women's Open

26.  1985 PGA Championship

27.  1985 U.S. Women's Open

28.  1985 U.S.G.A. Amateur

29.  Liberty Mutual Legends of Golf

30.  What was the site of Arnold Palmer's only U.S. Open victory?

31.  The largest island between Long Island and the Bahamas boasts 18 golf courses. What is its name?

32.  Jackie Gleason's "...and away we go!" is reminiscent of what Florida resort?

33.  The "Great American Chocolate Bar" and a round of golf on one of the three 18-hole championship courses makes what Pocono resort a perfect vacation spot?

34.  What golf course architect's signature is railroad ties?

35.  Where is "Hell's Half-Acre"?

36.  Where was the infamous par 3 pot bunker so deep that players entered and left via a ladder?

37.  The most common fairway grass on southern U.S. courses is what?

38. Why is there generally more backspin imparted by iron shots hit on southern courses?

39. Most northern U.S. courses use various strains of what grass on their fairways?

40. Where is the Swilcan Burn?

41. What was the first golf club established outside of Scotland?

42. Name the golf course Arnold Palmer represents on the Tour?

43. What is the name of the the first 18-hole course in the U.S. — opened in 1893?

44. What is the highest golf course in the world?

45. What body of water guards the famed 12th at Augusta National?

46. Who is Bob Baldock?

47. Who is Geoffry Cornish?

48. What designer's *piéce de résistance* is the Lower Course at Baltusrol, New Jersey?

49. What New England course, designed by Donald Ross, had Harold "Jug" McSpaden for its pro in the late 1930s and early 1940s?

50. What public course is the site of the Andy Williams San Diego Open?

51. The colonists would be proud of these Robert Trent Jones courses — one 9-hole and the lovely Golden Horseshoe Golf Course — located in the political capital of the colonies. Name the resort.

52. Where is the Barry Burn?

53. What is the home of the "Tin Whistles"?

54. Who is the 1985 recipient of the Green Section Award and developer of the Santa Ana strain of Bermuda grass?

55. Where is the "Valley of Sin"?

56. Founded in 1977, what 36-hole event is played on several courses in Vail, Colorado?

57. Name the first country club in the U.S.

58. Name the first golf club established in England.

59. Where is the southernmost golf course in the world?

60. Where is the northernmost golf course in the world?

77

61. Nestled in the rolling hills of northern Michigan, this resort offers the Heather Golf Course — rated in the "Top 100" by *Golf Digest* magazine — and the Moor Golf Links. What is it?

62. "The Brute" and "The Briar Patch" are challenging golf courses at what lakeside resort?

63. What edifice houses a collection of golf memorabilia, including President Eisenhower's golf cart?

64. What honeymooners' resort overlooking the Atlantic offers a scenic 18-hole Robert Trent Jones course?

65. What U.S. Open course names its nines "The Squirrel," "The Clyde," and "The Primrose"?

66. True or False: The Merion Golf Club uses wicker baskets instead of flags at the top of its pins.

67. Whose "Festival of Golf," held at the Dorado Beach Hotel, consists of 25 touring pros coming together to raise funds for the handicapped children of Puerto Rico?

68. What municipal golf course hosted the famous "Lucky (Strikes) International" for years?

69. How many U.S. courses were designed by Donald Ross?

70. Where is the World Golf Hall of Fame?

71. What is the location of Golf House, the U.S.G.A. headquarters?

72. Name the three golf courses played during the Bing Crosby Tournament.

73. True or False: The U.S. Open has been held at the Country Club, Brookline, Massachusetts three times.

74. What is the name of each nine at Sea Island Golf Club, Sea Island, Georgia?

75. Where is the Road Hole, the infamous 17th on the Old Course?

76. The Golden Isles of Georgia consist of three islands. Name them.

77. What is the oldest course west of the Mississippi?

78. What is the course record at the Riviera Country Club?

79. Name the city where Robert de Vicenzo learned to play golf.

80. What is the only golf club in China?

81. What was the original name of the Royal Calcutta Golf Club in India?

82. What was the site of the 1949 and 1975 U.S. Opens?

83. Where did Nicklaus shoot an 82 in 1976?

84. Who is the architect of the Mid-Ocean Course in Bermuda?

85. Who are the designers of Cypress Creek and Jack Rabbit at the Champion Golf Club in Texas?

86. What 625-yard 16th is often called "The Monster"?

87. Who coined the phrase "the white faces of Merion"?

88. Where is "Beman's Road"?

89. What is the last official event on the 1985 PGA tour?

90. Where was the 1985 PGA Assistant Professional Championship held?

91. Name the architect who designed Pinehurst #2.

92. What is the home of Maggie Leonard's cow that devoured hundreds of golf balls?

93. What is the nickname for the 3-hole stretch from the 11th to 13th holes at Augusta?

94. Who owned Baltusrol before it was purchased by Louis Keller, the owner of *The New York Social Register*?

95. What was the site of Fleck's 1955 U.S. Open upset over Hogan and Casper's 1966 win over Palmer?

96. What course was once called "the best 17-hole course in the world" by Jimmy Demaret?

97. What was the site of the 1957 Canada Cup?

98. What was the site of the first Canada Cup in 1953?

99. Who was the golf course designer for Cypress Point?

100. What Philadelphia hotelier designed Pine Valley?

101. Where is the "Principal's Nose" located?

102. What famous sea-side course was designed by two amateur golfers — their first effort?

103. A plaque honors R.T. Jones' British Open winning shot on the 17th hole of what famous course?

104. Where was the 1985 Canadian Open played?

105. In the 1920s it was billed as "The Workingman's Country Club." Name the course, designed by Donald Ross.

106. Where was the first "For Women Only" course established?

107. What is the number of Pinehurst's most famous course?

108. What great test of golf was created by George Crump as a protest against the presence of women at golf clubs?

109. What West Virginia resort did Sam Snead represent?

110. What was the site of Isoa Aoki's "miracle eagle"?

111. What famous resort was built because a wealthy member could not get preferred tee times at the Atlantic City Country Club?

112. Name the tourney hosted by Arnold Palmer.

113. What is the site of the 1988 U.S. Women's Amateur?

114. What was *Golf Digest's* "Best New Course of 1983"?

115. Where was Lee Trevino's 1984 PGA win?

116. What is the site of the 1987 U.S. Women's Open?

117. What is the site of *Golf World's* Inaugural Presidential Cup?

118. What was the site of the 1985 British Open?

119. What course was described by former U.S.G.A. President Sandy Tatum as "The Sistine Chapel of Golf"?

120. What hotel built the first hotel golf course in North America?

121. Who designed the Tournament Players Club at Sawgrass, Florida?

122. The Cascades is one of three famous courses at what Virginia resort?

123. What 18th has the largest water hazard in the world?

124. At how many different sites has the Tournament Players Championship been played since its inception in 1974? Bonus: Name them.

Each of the following is a name of a hole at the Augusta National. For each flower or tree name, give the number of the hole:

125. Yellow Jasmine

126. Flowering Crabapple

127. White Dogwood

128. Firethorn

129. Redbud

130. Flowering Peach

131. Camellia

132. Azalea

133. Tea Olive

83

134.  Holly

135.  Juniper

136.  Nandina

137.  Carolina Cherry

138.  Chinese Fir

139.  Golden Bell

140.  Pink Dogwood

141.  Magnolia

142.  Pampas

143.  What is the name of the oldest amateur golfing event in the U.S., and where is it held?

144.  This course, where Julius Boros is head pro, is host of the LPGA's Elizabeth Arden Classic. What is it?

145.  What is the famed golf resort area that will feature more than 50 golf courses by the end of 1986?

146.  What is the site of the Golf Writers of America Annual Tournament?

The following courses are ranked among the world's 170 best in the *World Atlas of Golf.* Give the location for each:

147.  Oak Hill Country Club

148.  Canterbury Golf Course

149. Peachtree Golf Course

150. Palmetto Dunes Resort

151. Dunes Golf and Beach Club

152. Juniper Hills Club

153. Cascades Golf Course

154. Quaker Ridge Golf Course

155. Prairie Dunes Golf Course

156. Scioto Golf Course

157. This famous resort hotel owns and operates the Sea Island Golf Club. Name it.

158. What Virgin Island resort features a course designed by George and Tom Fazio?

159. What well-known resort, located in Pine Mountain, Georgia, features four golf courses?

160. Its golf courses include Red Wing, Bow Creek, Kempsville Meadows, Stumpy Lake and Hell's Point. What is it?

161. This Phoenix, Arizona resort features three courses, two of which were designed by Robert Trent Jones. Name it.

162. What Tampa, Florida resort features 27 holes designed by Arnold Palmer and Dean Refram?

163. Tommy Armour and Sam Snead preceded Gary Wiren as what resort's head of golf instruction?

164. What location of a famous Indiana golf resort has been identified with basketball through the Boston Celtic's Larry Bird?

# PICTURES

1. The candy-striped lighhouse in the background should help you identify this famous course. What is it?

2. What two fairways are pictured?

A view looking across to the club house of the Concord Resort Hotel, Kiamesha Lake, New York.

3. Who designed the Concord Championship Course: (a) Robert Trent Jones (b) Donald Ross (c) Joseph S. Finger?

4. What is the nickname of the Championship Course?

5. How many holes does the Concord Resort Hotel Offer?

6. On Thursday Round in 1984, 64 pros found a watery grave on this 132-yard par 3. What was it?

7. How many holes from this same golf course are ranked among the toughest 18 on the PGA Tour, according to the 1984 PGA Tour statistics?

8. Name this course, located in the "Golf Capital of Pennsylvania" and designed by Maurice McCarthy.

9. What building is pictured?

10. What was the nickname of Henry Picard, resident pro from 1934 to 1941?

11. This rated as the lead-off course of the third 10 of America's finest golf courses by *Golf Digest* Magazine. What is it?

12. Who began his remarkable career here in 1935?

13. What other course at this Virginia resort boasts of having the oldest first tee in America — never changed since its inception in 1892?

14. The site of the 1985 U.S.G.A. Senior Amateur, this course has been rated as one of *Golf* Magazine's "50 Greatest Courses in the World" and *Golf Digest*'s "Top 100 Courses in the U.S." What is it?

15. What famous hole is pictured?

16. The four-year-old tournament played here boasts the unusual fact that its winners have earned *Golf Digest*'s number one ranking in their respective category each year. What is the name of the tournament?

17. This picture shows the site of the Tournament of Champions from 1953 to 1966. What is it?

18. What is the city in the background?

19. Which pro won the Tournament three years in a row when it was played here: Jerry Barber, Gene Littler, Jack Nicklaus, or Arnold Palmer?

20. What scenic, 425-yard, par 4 third hole is pictured?

21. What major amateur golf tournament is held here in 1985?

22. Constant onshore breezes from what body of water — combined with the flat landscape — make distance-judging difficult on this section of the course?

23. This picture shows the first clubhouse at a famous North Carolina golf resort. Name the resort.

24. What young Scottish golf professional is associated with the design and redesign of the four first courses here?

25. What Hall of Famer calls the No. 2 Course here "my No. 1 course"?

26. This is the 7th hole on the seaside nine of what Georgia golf course?

27. Name the ante-bellum cotton plantation on which all four nines of this course are located.

28. Give the distance and the par for this hole, listed regularly among the world's finest holes.

29. This course currently hosts the MONY Tournament of Champions. Name it.

30. What is the nickname of this famous 13th hole on the East Course of the Dorado Beach Golf resort in Dorado, Puerto Rico?

31. Who designed the course, and said this hole was one of his favorites?

32. The Amateur of the Americas Tournament held here draws participants from the U.S., the Caribbean, and Central and South America. What unique prizes are awarded to the winners?

33. Vieques Island is seen in the background from the 14th hole of the beautiful Palmas del Mar Resort in Humacao, Puerto Rico. Name the PGA Tour star who, along with Ron Kirby, designed this classic test of golf.

34. Palmas del Mar was designed as a playing counterpart to what other famous golf resort?

35. What is another name for, or slogan of, Palmas del Mar?

36. One of the U.S.'s top 50 courses, this resort hosts the Florida Golf Championship. Name the resort.

37. What famous hole is pictured?

38. What Philadelphia Phillies player makes his home on this island course?

39. An aerial view of a famous Miami resort with its guest lodges fanning out from the main clubhouse. Besides 2,400 lushly landscaped acres, the resort boasts four 18-hole, championship courses; 19 tennis courts; and a variety of other recreational amenities. Name the resort.

40. The great American novelist Henry James wrote of this resort: "...vast and cool and fair, friendly, breezy, shiny, swabbed and burnished like a royal yacht, really immaculate and delightful." What is it?

41. The facade and twin belvedere towers were inspired by what ancient European edifice?

42. What co-founder of Standard Oil conceived this resort?

43. This resort proclaims itself "The Resort That's a Way of Life." What is it?

44. In what year was this resort's first golf course, "The Lakeside," built?

45. In 1977, one of this resort's courses was redesigned by what golf great in preparation for its hosting the 1979 Ryder Cup?

103

46. Shown is the 18th green of the Golden Horseshoe Course of the Williamsburg Inn, Colonial Williamsburg. Who designed both golf courses at the Williamsburg Inn?

47. Why is this course named "The Golden Horseshoe"?

48. Who is the host for this championship course, resident pro and holder of the course record of 64 from the regular play tees?

49. This famous 13th hole TPC island green actually preceded its look-alike 17th hole at TPC Sawgrass. Where is it?

50. Pictured is the 11th hole on a course that was a former site of the TPC. Name the course.

51.  Identify this man.

# ANSWERS

# THE MAJORS

1. Double eagle on first day and double chip on the last day

2. Jackie Pung

3. The National Invitation Tournament

4. Juli Inkster

5. The cleek (4-wood); the Augusta National on the 15th hole

6. Sam Snead

7. 19 (Ray Ainsley, 1938)

8. They are all four-time runners-up.

9. Jack Fleck

10. Ben Crenshaw

11. Seve Ballesteros

12. Hollis Stacy

13. Walter Hagen

14. Nicklaus, 72; Sanders, 73

15. Gary Player (South Africa) and Kel Nagle (Australia)

16. Tony Jacklin (1970) and David Graham (1981)

17. Mildred Didrikson Zaharias; Atlantic City Country Club in 1948 and Rolling Hills in 1950

18. Walter Hagen (1922); three (1924, 1928 and 1929)

19. The British Amateur

20. The Masters and the PGA

21. Johnny McDermott (1911)

22. Bob Charles

23. Gary Player (289 total)

24. Harry Vardon

25. Interlachen Country Club in Edina, Minnesota

26. Mickey Wright with nine (four U.S. Opens, four LPGAs and one Dinah Shore)

27. Catherine Lacoste (1967)

28. Patty Berg (1946)

29. Gary Player (1961), Seve Ballesteros (1983) and Bernhard Langer (1985)

30.  Sam Snead — 44

31.  Jack Nicklaus at 46

32.  Seve Ballesteros at 23

33.  Gene Sarazen (1922) and Tom Creavy (1931)

34.  Julius Boros, who was 48 in 1968

35.  Beverly Hanson in 1955

36.  Ed Furgol

37.  Two — Jack Nicklaus (Balustrol Golf Course) and Willie Anderson (Myopia Hunt Club)

38.  Sam Snead

39.  Jack Nicklaus (1965 and 1966)

40.  Seve Ballesteros

41.  Four

42.  James Anderson (1878); 1877 and 1879

43.  One, the 1946 Championship

44.  Four (1923, 1926, 1929 and 1930)

45.  1 (d), 2 (e), 3 (c), 4 (b), 5 (a)

46.  The Green Jacket

47.  Julius Boros of Connecticut at The Country Club, Brookline, Massachusetts (1963)

48.  1958

49.  Each was a runner-up as an amateur.

50.  Palmer and Watson

51.  Roberto de Vicenzo — he had tied Bob Goalby for the winning score, but signed an incorrect scorecard.

52.  Ralph Guldahl

53.  Billy Casper

54.  Lee Trevino

55.  Harry Vardon and Ted Ray

56.  The 13th hole — he took a seven and dropped out of the tournament lead. Curtis Strange lost his lead by going into the same creek.

57.  Ayako Okamoto — 11 strokes

58.  Canterbury Golf Club, Cleveland, Ohio

59.  Lee Elder

60.  Seve Ballesteros

61.  Gary Player ($5,000 to cancer research and $20,000 to U.S.G.A. Junior golf)

62.  Six

63.  James Barnes

64. Johnny Miller's 63 at Merion in 1973

65. Lawson Little in 1934 and 1935

66. Gene Sarazen — the 8th at Troon, 1973

67. Thirteen strokes, by Tom Morris Senior in 1862

68. Jerry Barber

69. Bruce Crampton, Gary Player and Isao Aoki; Jack Nicklaus beat Crampton in 1972 and Aoki in 1980.

70. Clifford Roberts

71. Willie Anderson

72. Young Tom Morris

73. He was six over par after the first three holes.

74. Jones' Grand Slam

75. 1963

76. Jack Nicklaus — seven times (1964, 1967, 1968, 1972, 1976, 1977 and 1979)

77. 1917

78. The U.S. Amateur, the British Amateur, the U.S. Open and the British Open

79. Francis Ouimet

80. Jay and Lionel Herbert (1957 and 1960)

81. Hollis Stacy

82. The Dinah Shore

83. Six

84. Two U.S. Opens and two Du Maurier's

85. He beat Arnold Palmer in the 18-hole playoff.

86. The PGA

87. Ken Venturi

88. Ken Venturi

89. Byron Nelson

90. The 1942 PGA at the Seaview Country Club in Atlantic City

91. The U.S. Open

92. Dave Stockton

93. Six

94. Sam Snead and Lew Worsham

95. Gene Sarazen

96. Tony Jacklin

97. Tom Morris Senior and Junior

98.   St. Andrews; Prestwick (1860)

99.   Gene Sarazen

100.  Prestwick            Troon
      St. Andrews          Lytham
      Musselburgh          Carnoustie
      Hoylake              Prince's
      Sandwich             Portrush
      Muirfield            Birkdale
      Deal                 Turnberry

101.  Prestwick

102.  The U.S. PGA, the British Open, the U.S. Open and the Masters

103.  Horton Smith

104.  Five

105.  Willie Anderson

106.  Lloyd Mangrum

107.  Julius Boros

108.  Jim Foulis

109.  Merion; Lloyd Mangrum and George Fazio

110.  It was stolen on the walk from the 72nd green to the clubhouse, and never returned.

111.  David Ogrin

112.  Mickey Wright — nine

113. George Archer in 1983. His daughter caddied for him.

114. Bobby Jones

115. 18 — four U.S. Opens, three British Opens, six Masters and five PGAs

116. Eight — five British Opens, two Masters and one U.S. Open

117. Six — two U.S. Opens, two British Opens and two PGAs

118. Nine — three British Opens, three Masters, two PGAs and one U.S. Open

119. Nine — four U.S. Opens, two Masters, two PGAs and one British Open

120. 11 — four British Opens, two U.S. Opens and five PGAs

121. Seven — three PGAs, three Masters and one British Open

122. Seven — three PGAs, two U.S. Opens, one British Open and one Masters

123. Seven — four Masters, two British Opens and one U.S. Open

124. He studied mechanical engineering at Georgia Tech, earned a degree in English literature from Harvard, and passed his bar exam half-way through his second year of law school at Emory.

125. False

126. True

127. True

128. False

129. True

130. False — twice

131. True

132. False

133. False

134. True

135. False — Bobby Locke has as well.

136. False — Harry Vardon has, among others.

137. True

138. Kathy Baker

139. Tony Jacklin in 1969 at Royal Lytham and St. Anne's

140. The 1977 U.S. Open at Southern Hills

141. No

# THE MEDIA

1. Bob Hope

2. Ben Hogan about the New York ticker tape parade, 1953 (from *Great Moments in Golf* by Nevin H. Gibson)

3. Richard S. Taylor

4. Peter Alliss

5. Lew Worsham holed out a 130-yard wedge for an eagle to nose out Harper.

6. George Plimpton

7. Arnold Palmer

8. Pat Ward-Thomas

9. Carney waved and said, "Hello, ball!"

10. Jimmy D'Angelo (March, 1942; WPTZ — Chicago, Philco Station)

11.   Lee Trevino

12.   Joe Concannon

13.   William H. Davis

14.   According to Tom Michael in *Golfer's Digest,* Sam Snead's swing.

15.   Francis Ouimet

16.   Jess Sweetser, U.S. & British Amateur Champion

17.   Ken Venturi

18.   Jimmy Ballard

19.   Dave Hill and Nick Seitz

20.   CBS

21.   ESPN

22.   NBC

23.   CBS

24.   NBC

25.   ABC

26.   ABC

27.   Billy Casper (with Al Barkow)

28.   *Murder on the Links*

29.   Scott Verplank

30. Lee Trevino (*Golf World* Magazine, Dec. 1984)

31. *Golf* Magazine

32. Herbert Warren Wind

33. Bob Toski

34. Jimmy Demaret

35. Walter Hagen

36. *The Haunted Bridge*

37. Jack Burke, Jr.

38. *Goldfinger*

39. Arnold Palmer

40. Charles Price

41. O.B. Keeler

42. 1953 World Championship at Tam O'Shanter, Chicago. With its $25,000 first prize, it was the granddaddy of today's rich Tour.

43. Michael Murphy

44. James P. Lee, *Golf in America* (1895)

45. Ben Hogan

46. Doug Ford

47. Jack Nicklaus

48. Barry McDermott

49. Arnold Palmer

50. Brent Musburger

51. Peter Alliss

52. NBC

53. NBC

54. ABC-TV

55. *The New Yorker*

56. Tony Lema with Gwilyn S. Brown

57. Jack Whitaker

58. Pat Summerall

59. Henry Longhurst

60. Dave Marr

61. Babe Zaharias

62. John Brodie

63. *Down the Fairway*

64. *Fairway*

65. Bob Rosburg

66. Dinah Shore

67.   CBS

68.   Jimmy Demaret

69.   Susan Clark; Alex Karras

70.   Ronald Reagan

71.   Lee Trevino

72.   Jim Barnes

73.   Larry Cirillo

74.   Ben Wright

75.   Henry Cotton

76.   Barbara Romack

77.   Bob Bruno; Abe

78.   Lee Trevino

79.   Nancy Lopez with Peter Schwed

80.   Frank Chirkinian

81.   Tommy Bolt with Jimmy Mann

82.   Vin Scully

83.   NBC

84.   Jack Nicklaus with Ken Bowden

85.   Tom Weiskopf

86.   Herbert Warren Wind

87.   Ken Venturi

88.   True

89.   ESPN

90.   Bruce Devlin

91.   False — Tom Roy is the golf producer for NBC.

92.   Clive Clark

93.   Yes

94.   *Five Lessons: The Modern Fundamentals of Golf* (with Herbert Warren Wind)

95.   *Sports Illustrated*

96.   (a) — James was then managing editor of *Sports Illustrated* and Barnes was the book's publisher.

97.   John Brodie; No, he missed by one stroke.

98.   True

99.   Bernhard Langer

# THE PROS

1.  Dentist

2.  Mark O'Meara (-5)

3.  Tom Watson, Gary Player, Jack Nicklaus, and Arnold Palmer; Palmer was the winner from all the carry-overs.

4.  Craig Stadler

5.  Byron Nelson with 113

6.  Billy Casper

7.  DeWitt Weaver

8.  Frank Urban Zoeller

9.  Nancy Lopez, with five in 1978

10. Tom Watson ($530,808 in 1980)

11. Al Geiberger

12. Sally Little

13. Marlene Floyd

14. Ralph Terry

15. Greg Norman, Bruce Crampton, and David Graham

16. Patty Berg and Babe Zaharias

17. Dave Hill

18. Jim Gallagher, Jr. ($70,857)

19. He is an optometrist.

20. Jon Fiedler

21. JoAnne Carner

22. Al Balding and George Knudson

23. Peter Oosterhuis

24. Ben Hogan

25. 290; Jan Stephenson at the GNA Classic in 1985 and Hollis Stacy at the U.S. Women's Open in 1984

26. Jim Thorpe (over Jack Renner)

27. Soozi and Rose Nelson

28. $6,767

29. Wiffy Cox and Wiffi Smith (LPGA)

30. Ed Dougherty (Pennsylvania)

31. JoAnne Carner

32. Byron Nelson with 11

33. Walter Hagen

34. Tom Morris, Sr. (1821-1908)

35. The 1949 Motor City Open in Detroit, where 11 extra holes where played by Lloyd Mangrum and Cary Middlecoff. Neither man won, as the match was stopped on account of darkness; they were declared co-champions.

36. Kermit Zarley

37. Don Cherry

38. Legendary golf hustler

39. The 1962 U.S. Open

40. Chi Chi Rodriguez

41. Arnold Palmer

42. Lee Trevino

43. Ben Hogan

44. Lee Trevino

45. Bob Toski

46. Dave Stockton (Richard Stockton)

47. Deacon

48. Barry Jaeckel (Richard Jaeckel)

49. Jack Nicklaus — 105 feet

50. Nabisco Dinah Shore Invitational ($400,000)

51. Sam Snead

52. Mike Souchak

53. Last in the money with $33.33

54. Mark O'Meara

55. Brad Faxon

56. Al Geiberger

57. Billy Casper

58. Brad Bryant

59. Jack Nicklaus

60. Dennis Watson

61. Lee Trevino

62. Gene Sarazen

63. Al Besselink — $10,000 in silver dollars

64. Frank Conner

65. Seve Ballesteros

66. John Jacobs (USA)

67. Alexander Walter Barr Lyle

68. Calvin Peete with 274

69. Jay Haas

70. Gibby Gilbert

71. Bob Toski

72. Pat Bradley

73. Phil Blackmar

74. Although she ranked fourth on the year's money list and was a runner-up four times and third four times, she never won.

75. Mildred Didrikson Zaharias

76. Lionel and Jay Hebert, Dave and Danny Edwards, Ted and Ed Furgol, Mike and Dave Hill, Tom and Joe Lally, and Jim and Walter Turnesa

77. Chi Chi Rodriguez

78. Andrew Magee (born May 22, 1962)

79. Calvin Peete

80. Arnold Palmer

81. Cary Middlecoff

82. He is Sam's nephew.

83. Ron Cerrudo

84. Johnny Miller

85. Paul Runyan

86. Bob Murphy

87. Johnny Miller

88. Highest winning score of the year (280)

89. William E. Mehlhorn

90. Betty Jameson, Louise Suggs, Babe Zaharias and Patty Berg

91. Doug Sanders

92. Harold McSpaden

93. Judy Rankin (1976)

94. Sandra Palmer

95. Tony Lema

96. Ken Venturi

97. Althea Gibson

98. Nancy Lopez-Knight (husband Ray Knight)

99. Laura Baugh Cole and Bobby Cole

100. Gene Littler

101. Julius Boros

102. Mike Souchak

103. Hal Sutton

104. Ky Laffoon

105. Kathy Whitworth (87)

106. Sam Snead (84 since 1937)

107. Bob Goalby (1961 St. Petersburg Open) and Fuzzy Zoeller (1976 Quad Cities Open) — both with eight

108. Ben Hogan

109. Jack Grout

110. Beverly Klass, who was ten years old in 1967

111. Harry E. Cooper

112. Clayton Heafner

113. Sam Byrd

114. Fred Haas

115. Hal Sutton

116. Lanny Wadkins

117. Jack Nicklaus

118. Raymond Floyd

119. Lanny Wadkins. He beat Craig Stadler.

120. Tommy Armour

121. Don January

122. Byron Nelson

123. Eight

124. Colonial National Invitation

125.  Ky Laffoon (1934, 1935 and 1938)

126.  Roberto de Vicenzo

127.  Tom Kite (275, 13 under par)

128.  Arnold Palmer

129.  Bill Ezinicki

130.  Muffin Spencer-Devlin with a 28 at Mastercard

131.  Miller Barber

132.  Tom Kite

133.  Danny Edwards (Ketchcan, Alaska)

134.  Billy Casper

135.  Buck

136.  Larry Nelson

137.  Paul Harney

138.  Mark McNulty

139.  $620

140.  Jacqueline Pung

141.  Jim Colbert

142.  Calvin Peete

143.  Peter Jacobsen and D.A. Weibring

144.  Gil Morgan

145. Johnny Miller

146. Joe Kirkwood ("over" 5,000)

147. Evan "Big Cat" Williams (1976 and 1977)

148. "Porky"

149. Walter Hagen (U.S.) and Ted Ray (England)

150. Julius Boros

151. He sold insurance.

152. Art Wall, Jr. (37)

153. Betsy King ($266,771)

154. Gay Brewer and Billy Casper

155. Jack Nicklaus ($4,686,280)

156. Peter Thompson ($386,724)

157. Roberto de Vicenzo

158. Jesse Guilford

159. Percentage of subpar holes (.220 in '84 and .218 in '85)

160. Craig Stadler

161. Andy Bean

162. Don Pooley (70.36 average)

163. Fuzzy Zoeller

164. George Archer

165. Sandy Lyle

166. Thomas Bolt

167. Lary Rinker (14)

168. Lanny Wadkins

169. Greg Norman

170. Joey Sindelar (411)

171. Kathy Whitworth

172. Nancy Lopez (70.73)

173. Gene Sarazen

174. 1956 Egyptian PGA

175. Eight consecutive birdies

176. Ky Laffoon

177. Jack Nicklaus

178. Fuzzy Zoeller

179. A mexican hat

180. Chi Chi Rodriguez

181. Horton Smith

182. Arnold Palmer

183. Ralph Guldahl

184. Byron Nelson

185. Byron Nelson and Jug McSpaden

186. Ben Hogan

187. Tony Jacklin

188. Bob Charles

189. Palmer, Nicklaus, and Player

190. Orville Moody or Walter Burkemo

191. Larry and Laurie Rinker (66-68-67-66-267)

192. Al Balding (1955 Mayfair Inn Open)

193. Jimmy Ballard

194. Sewsunker Sewgolum. He held his left hand below his right.

195. 1953 — he entered five tournaments and won all five.

196. The Masters, the Pan-American Open, the U.S. Open, the Colonial National Open, and the British Open

197. Ballesteros (USF & G Classic)

198. Ernest Joseph Harrison

199. Juan

200. The 1954 World Championship; Bob Toski

201. The Tam O'Shanter Country Club, Chicago

202. John Mahaffey (.719)

203. Lanny Wadkins, 7 strokes in Los Angeles

204. a) 6, b) 7, c) 1, d) 8, e) 2, f) 3, g) 5, h) 9, i) 4

205. A red jacket

206. Marta Figueras-Dotti

207. 1 (e), 2 (c), 3 (b), 4 (d), 5 (a)

208. Hale Irwin

209. Mickey Powell

210. The Army Air Corps

211. Panasonic-Las Vegas Invitational — $950,000

212. Jack Nicklaus

213. 1962

214. Course architect Peter Dye and tour commissioner Deane Beman

215. At Memphis after winning the Danny Thomas Memphis Classic

216. Putting

217. Jim Nelford

218. Arthur D'Arcy "Bobby" Locke

219. Arnold Palmer

220. 1960

221. 1 (c), 2 (a), 3 (b), 4 (d)

222. Mancil Davis

223. Sam Snead

224. Bobbie Jones

225. 1957

# THE AMATEURS

1.  14

2.  393 yards on the first hole at the Furnace Brook Golf course in 1949

3.  British Amateur

4.  George H. Walker

5.  Harriet and Margaret

6.  Bobby Jones

7.  Its Centennial, June 3-8 in Royal Dornoch, Scotland

8.  Yale University (21 times)

9.  Scott Verplank

10. False

11. False

12. True (1975)

13. False

14. True (1947)

15. True (1938)

16. True (1952)

17. True (1969)

18. "The President's Putter" between the Oxford and Cambridge Golfing Societies

19. Michael Bonallack

20. Juli Inkster

21. Doug Sanders (1956)

22. Glenna Collett Vare

23. Nicklaus — Ohio State; Palmer — Wake Forest; and Watson — Stanford

24. Walter J. Travis (1904)

25. Harold Hilton

26. George Von Elm

27. Illinois

28. San Jose State, California

29. Tulsa

30. University of Florida

31. University of Texas

32. Brigham Young

33 Ohio State

34. Oregon

35. Southern Optometry

36. Rollins

37. Alabama

38. UCLA

39. University of Southern California

40. Centenary College

41. Oklahoma State

42. University of Houston

43. Notre Dame

44. Holy Cross

45. North Texas State

46. Oklahoma

47. Hales Secretarial

48. Lawson Little

49. Houston

50. Francis Ouimet (1913), J.D. Travers (1915), Chick Evans Jr. (1916), Bobby Jones (1923, 1926, 1929, 1930), and J. G. Goodman (1933)

51. John G. Goodman (1933)

52. Ben Crenshaw

53. Five

54. Jay Sigel

55. Eight

56. Walter Travis

57. 1922

58. Duffy Waldorf

59. Babe Zaharias

60. False

61. True (1967)

62. False

63. True (1970)

64. True (1961)

65. False

66. True (1971-1973)

67. True (1972)

68. True (1920)

69. False

70. False

71.  True (1962)

72.  False

73.  False

74.  False

75.  False

76.  False

77.  True (1976)

78.  Ken Venturi

79.  Joanne Carner

80.  Janet Anderson

81.  3,625 by Ralph Kennedy, N.Y.C.

82.  Jack Nicklaus

83.  Bob Murphy

84.  Newport, Rhode Island (1895)

85.  1938

86.  The United States

87.  They have each won the PGA Long Drive Championship (in 1975, 1978 and 1979, respectively).

88.  The Fred Haskins Award

89.  Dana Lofland, Oknard, Calif.

90.  Charles Rymer

91.  Edward S. Stimpson

92.  28

93.  Danielle Ammaccapane

94.  Glenna Collett Vare; six

95.  Virginia Van Wie

96.  True — in 1946

97.  False

98.  True

99.  False — he won at Olympic.

100.  True — in 1972

101.  True — 1963

102.  False

103.  False

104.  False

105.  Walter J. Travis

106.  Jerry Travers

107.  Louise Suggs

108.  Bob Sweeney

109.  Laura Baugh

110.   Bob Dickson

111.   True (from 1956-1966)

112.   1971

113.   Scott Verplank, 1985 Western Open

114.   Michiko Hattori

115.   Lew Oehmig

# THE EQUIPMENT

1. True

2. Surlyn and balata

3. Coburn Haskell, Cleveland, Ohio

4. A caddy's foot that kicks balls from bad lies

5. Throwing the ball with your hand

6. 1948

7. A primitive golf ball consisting of a leather sphere stuffed with feathers

8. #10

9. Old names for golf clubs

10. "Brassie"

11. "Spoon"

12. "Cleek"

13. "Driving iron"

14. "Midiron"

15. "Mid-mashie"

16. "Mashie"

17. "Spade mashie"

18. "Mashie niblick"

19. "Lofter"

20. "Niblick"

21. Soaking overnight in a bucket of water

22. Hickory

23. Chick Evans

24. Izod Lacoste

25. Knickerbocker-like slacks worn four inches below the knee

26. Karsten Solheim

27. A 6-iron

28. Gary Player with "Shakespeare" shafts

29. The hosel is located where the clubhead joins the shaft.

30. AT&T

31. $11\frac{1}{2}^{0}$

32. A pinch of sand

33. Wedgy Winchester, 319 yds, 14"; he used an extra-long club.

34. A Gutta-Percha golf ball

35. A rubber golf ball. This marked the national introduction of the Haskell rubber golf ball; Travis was the only player in a field of 20 using it.

36. Chi Chi Rodriguez

37. Spalding Tour Edition Clubs

38. "Featherlites"

39. Hogan

40. Ram

41. Sounder

42. Hillerich & Bradsbury Co.'s Century Collection Clubs

43. Hogan

44. Cobra

45. Peerless, by Pro Group, Inc.

46. Wilson Staff

47. Ram

48. Northwestern

49. Balata

50. Walter Hagen

51. Acushnet Company

52. Wilson

53. Titleist

54. MacGregor

55. False

56. Taylor-Made

57. Spalding

58. Foot-Joy

59. Bobby Jones' wooden shafted putter

60. After putting out, from the cup of the previous hole

61. Seven wooden shafted clubs: brassie, spoon, midiron, jigger, lofter, niblick and putter

62. Gutta-Percha

63. E.F. Hutton

64. Cadillac

65. Northwestern

66. United Van Lines

67. 492

68. Pinseeker

69. A device for measuring the speed of greens

70. 432

71. Dunlop

72. Rolex

73. Taylor-Made Golf Co.

74. Daiwa Golf Company

75. Spalding

76. Dunlop's "Master"

77. The machine used by the U.S.G.A. to determine whether a manufacturer's ball exceeds allowable specifications

78. Dexter

79. Bostonian

80. False — It is located in Norcross, Georgia.

# TRIVIAL TRIVIA

1. Fort Worth, Texas

2. John Laupheimer

3. Mark McCormack

4. Fred Corcoran

5. George Low

6. Arnold Palmer's caddie for his four Masters victories

7. Creamy Carolyn

8. Commissioner of the Men's Tour

9. Joseph C. Dey

10. 1973

11. Tom Weiskopf (wife Jeanne)

12. Jim Hand of Ossining, New York

13. Three, by Dr. Joseph Boydstone of Bakersfield, California

14. Evan Williams who, in 1977, drove 353 yards, 23 inches

15. 515 yards by Mike Austin at the 1974 National Seniors Open

16. Craig Wood with 430 yards on the 5th hole at St. Andrews, the 1933 British Open

17. A St. Albans seed merchant who donated the Ryder Cup

18. Barbara

19. Robert Tyre Jones Jr.

20. It is given by the PGA of America Advisory Committee to a professional whose contribution to the field of professional education is outstanding.

21. Edward E. "Eddie" Lowery

22. Jack Tuthill

23. Valerie

24. Fred Corcoran

25. George S. May

26. Norman Mancy (54)

27. He shot his age (64).

28. Holly

29. Joe Kirkwood

30. Gerald Ford

31. Dwight Eisenhower

32. Men no, women yes

33. William Howard Taft

34. *"Der Meisterswinger"*

35. Ben Hogan, Sam Snead, and Byron Nelson were all born in 1912.

36. No

37. 1922

38. Oldsmobile

39. Greens hit in regulation

40. King Edward VIII

41. Putting with a billiard cue; Charles B. MacDonald

42. The Wanamaker Trophy

43. A conceded putt

44. Players are dispersed around the 18 holes and start together (at the sound of a shotgun), thereby finishing at the same time.

45. All players in the group play a shot, and the best is chosen. This is repeated into the hole and on succeeding holes.

46. 1916

47. The Radix

48. 50

49. The Caddy Scholarship Fund

50. Those of championship length

51. Women, with 40

52. The Canadian Cup

53. On a par 3, a ball that lands on the green

54. 1904

55. Most tournaments were match play, and players walked 36 holes per day.

56. He gets paid for telling people "where to go."

57. An early French game similar to golf

58. Monday qualifiers on the PGA Tour

59. Lee Trevino was struck by lightning.

60. A double eagle, or albatross

61. Harry Vardon

62. 1951

63. $300

64. With horse-drawn gang mowers

65. A double bogey

66. Match play is by the total holes won; medal play is by total strokes.

67. Over 575 yards

68. $9.4 million

69. A hole-in-one

70. NBC ended coverage of the 1985 Hope Classic at playoff time to show the sitcom "Silver Spoons."

71. 1976

72. Five: Gary, Nan, Steven, Michael and Jack William II

73. 10,331 to 1

74. Vare Trophy

75. August Busch (Budweiser)

76. Lowest scoring average

77. *Cadet* — "pupils" or "attendant"

78. Francis Ouimet

79. Mary, Queen of Scots

80. The drive he hit off the top of the Eiffel Tower

81. "Inside the leather" — a "gimme" put

82. President Gerald Ford

83. No, he failed in the attempt.

84. Peter Dobereiner

85. One

86. Don't ask!

87. At the Atlantic City Country Club, when Abner Smith hit a "bird of a shot"

88. Willie Park Jr., two-time winner of the British Open in the 1880s, and said by many to have been the best putter of all time; the term refers to putting.

89. The balls weigh 17 and 20 grams, with compressions of 30 to 50. Regulation balls weigh 45, 93 grams with 80 to 100 compressions.

90. A man/woman team hitting alternate shots

91. 72

92. Ten par 4s, four par 5s and four par 3s (5, 2 and 2 each 9)

93. The Breakers

94. Dorado Beach Hotel

95. Colonial Williamsburg

96.  Sea Pines Plantation

97.  La Costa

98.  14,000,000

99.  St. Andrews in Ardsley, New York (1888)

100. John Reid

101. Scotland and the Netherlands

102. Scotland

103. Royal Montreal Golf Club (1873)

104. Shinnecock Hills in Southhampton, Long Island

105. George Wright of Boston

106. Samuel Parrish of Shinnecock Hills

107. Ralph "Cooney" Weiland

108. Jerome Travers

109. Walter J. Travis

110. Curtis Cup, Walker Cup and Ryder Cup

111. Ken Harrelson

112. The award given annually by the Golf Writers Association of America to the individual who has made consistently outstanding contributions to golf

113. The award given by the National Golf Foundation for contribution to golf education with emphasis on juniors

114. Paul Runyan

115. Bob Hope Desert Classic and the Panasonic Las Vegas Invitational

116. True

117. True

118. True

119. Yes — he was in the U.S. Coast Guard from 1951 to 1954.

120. Gary Player — he claims it gives him strength.

121. Hershey, Pennsylvania (with 72 holes on five courses, all within a few blocks of the center of town)

122. "Gloria"

# THE COURSES

1. Rolling Hills Golf Resort in Ft. Lauderdale, Florida

2. Worcester, Massachusetts (1927)

3. Wayzata Country Club, Minnesota

4. Wild Dunes

5. Ocean, Sea-Marsh and Harbor Town Golf Links

6. Casa de Campo, Dominican Republic

7. The Red, White, Gold and Green Courses

8. La Costa Hotel and Spa

9. Royal St. George, Sandwich, England

10. Newport Country Club, Newport, Rhode Island

11. Pleasant Valley Country Club, Sutton, Massachusetts

12. Congressional Country Club, Bethesda, Maryland

13. Harbour Town Golf Links, Hilton Head Island, South Carolina

14. Radisson Ferncroft Country Club, Danvers, Massachusetts

15. Mission Hills Country Club, Rancho Mirage, California

16. La Costa Country Club, Carlsbad, California

17. Tournament Players Club, Ponte Vedra, Florida

18. PGA National Golf Course (Champion Course), Palm Beach Garden, California

19. Butler National Golf Course, Oak Brook, Illinois

20. Firestone Country Club, Akron, Ohio

21. Pinehurst Country Club, Pinehurst, North Carolina

22. The Country Club, Brookline, Massachusetts

23. Oakland Hills Country Club, Birmingham, Michigan

24. Jack Nicklaus Sports Center, Kings Island, Ohio

25. Salem Country Club, Peabody, Massachusetts

26. Cherry Hill Country Club, Englewood (Denver), Colorado

27. Baltusrol Golf Course, Springfield, New Jersey

28. Montclair Golf Course, Montclair, New Jersey

29. Onion Creek Country Club, Austin, Texas

30. Cherry Hill Country Club, Denver, Colorado

31. Hilton Head

32. Innisbrook

33. Hotel Hershey & Country Club

34. Pete Dye

35. The 7th at Pine Valley, New Jersey

36. Harbour Town, Hilton Head

37. Bermuda grass

38. Because of shorter grass on the fairways

39. Bent grass

40. St. Andrews, Scotland

41. The Calcutta Golf Club of East India (1829)

42. Bay Hill Country Club

43. The Chicago Golf Club

44. Tucta Golf Club in Peru — 14,335 feet above sea level

45. Rae's Creek

46. The recipient of the National Golf Foundation's Outstanding Service Award, and architect of 350 courses all over the country

47. The designer of more than 100 courses in New England

48. Arthur W. Tillinghast

49. Winchester Country Club, Winchester, Massachusetts

50. Torrey Pines, La Jolla, California

51. Colonial Williamsburg

52. Carnoustie, Scotland

53. Pinehurst Country Club, Pinehurst, North Carolina

54. Dr. Victor B. Youngner

55. The 18th at St. Andrews

56. The Jerry Ford Invitational Golf Tournament

57. The Country Club, Brookline, Massachusetts

58. The Golf Club of Westward Ho (Devonshire, 1864)

59.  The Falkland Islands Stanley Club, Port Stanley

60.  Lapland

61.  Boyne Highlands

62.  Americana Lake Geneva Resort

63.  World Golf Hall of Fame

64.  Castle Harbour Hotel, Beach, Golf and Racquet Club

65.  The Country Club, Brookline, Massachusetts

66.  True, except during the winter

67.  Chi Chi Rodriguez's

68.  Harding Park, San Francisco, California

69.  Approximately 600

70.  Pinehurst, North Carolina

71.  Far Hills, New Jersey

72.  Pebble Beach, Spy Glass Hill, and Cypress Point

73.  False — only twice, in 1913 and 1963

74.  "Seaside," "Plantation," "Retreat," and "Marshside"

75.  St. Andrews, Scotland

76. Jekyll Island, St. Simons Island and Sea Island

77. Del Monte Golf Course, Monterey, California

78. 62 by Larry Mize (1985 L.A. Open)

79. Buenos Aires

80. The Royal Hong Kong

81. Dum Dum Golfing Club

82. Medinah Country Club, Chicago, Illinois

83. Pebble Beach

84. Charles Blair Macdonald

85. Jimmy Demaret and Jackie Burke

86. Firestone Country Club, Akron, Ohio

87. Chick Evans in 1916 at the U.S. Amateur; he was referring to deep sand traps.

88. It borders the 15th at Merion, where Deane Beman went out-of-bounds in the 1966 U.S. Amateur.

89. Chrysler Team Invitational (Dec. 13-16, Boca Raton, Florida)

90. Thorny Lea Golf Club, Brockton, Massachusetts

91. Donald Ross

92. Portmarnock Golf Club, County Dublin, Ireland

93. "Amen Corner"

94. Mr. Baltus Roll

95. Olympic Country Club in San Francisco

96. Cypress Point Club, Pebble Beach, California

97. Kasumigaseki Country Club, Tokyo, Japan

98. Montreal, Quebec

99. Dr. Alister MacKenzie

100. George Crump

101. The 16th at St. Andrews

102. Pebble Beach — designed by Jack Neville and Douglas Grant

103. Royal Lytham

104. Oakville, Ontario

105. George Wright Municipal, Hyde Park, Massachusetts

106. Morris County, New Jersey

107. #2

108. Pine Valley, Clementon, New Jersey

109. The Greenbrier

110. The 18th at the 1983 Hawaiian Open — he holed a wedge to beat Jack Renner by one shot.

111. Seaview Country Club, Absecon, New Jersey

112. Bay Hill Classic

113. Minikohda Club, Minneapolis, Minnesota

114. Sentry World, Stevens Point, Wisconsin

115. Shoal Creek, Alabama

116. Plainfield Country Club, Plainfield, New Jersey

117. Grand Cypress Resort/Hyatt Regency Complex, Orlando, Florida

118. Royal St. George, Sandwich, England

119. Cypress Point

120. The Lake Champlain Hotel

121. Pete Dye

122. The Homestead

123. Pebble Beach (alongside the Pacific)

124. Five: Atlanta Country Club, Atlanta, Georgia; Colonial Country Club, Fort Worth, Texas; Inverrary Golf &

Country Club, Lauderhill, Florida;
Sawgrass, Ponte Vedra, Florida;
Tournament Players Club, Ponte
Vedra, Florida.

125.  8th

126.  4th

127.  11th

128.  15th

129.  16th

130.  3rd

131.  10th

132.  13th

133.  1st

134.  18th

135.  6th

136.  17th

137.  9th

138.  14th

139.  12th

140.  2nd

141.  5th

142.  7th

143. Men's North and South Amateur Invitation, Pinehurst Country Club, North Carolina

144. Turnberry Island Country Club, Miami, Florida

145. Myrtle Beach, South Carolina

146. Dunes Golf and Beach Club, Myrtle Beach, South Carolina

147. Rochester, New York

148. Cleveland, Ohio

149. Atlanta, Georgia

150. Hilton Head Island, South Carolina

151. Myrtle Beach, South Carolina

152. Tequesta, Florida

153. Hot Springs, Virginia

154. Scarsdale, New York

155. Hutchinson, Kansas

156. Columbus, Ohio

157. The Cloister Hotel, Sea Island, Georgia

158. Mahogany Run Golf and Tennis Resort, St. Thomas, U.S. Virgin Islands

159. Callaway Gardens

160. Virginia Beach

161. The Wigwam

162. Saddlebrook

163. The Boca Raton Hotel and Club, Boca Raton, Florida

164. French Lick, Indiana

# PICTURES

1. Harbour Town Golf Links at Sea Pines Plantation, Hilton Head Island, South Carolina

2. The first and the ninth

3. Joseph S. Finger of Houston, Texas

4. "The Monster" (7,205 yards)

5. 45 in all

6. The 17th at the Tournament Players Club, Sawgrass, Ponte Vedra, Florida

7. Two — the 18th, a 440-yard par 4; and the 9th a 582-yard par 5

8. The 5th hole on Hershey Country Club's West Course

9. Chocolate manufacturer Milton S. Hershey's High Point Mansion — today a registered national landmark and corporate headquarters of Hershey Foods Corporation

10. "The Chocolate Soldier"

11. The first tee of the Cascades Course of the Homestead Resort

12. Sam Snead — it was his first professional victory.

13. The Homestead Course

14. Wild Dunes Golf Links

15. 18th

16. Wild Dunes Senior Invitational Golf Tournament

17. Desert Inn Country Club

18. Las Vegas, Nevada

19. Gene Littler (1955-1957)

20. New Seabury's Blue Course

21. National Collegiate Women's Golf Championship

22. Nantucket Sound

23. Pinehurst Hotel & Country Club

24. Donald J. Ross

25. Sam Snead

26. Sea Island, The Cloister, Sea Island, Georgia

27. Retreat Plantation

28. 435 yards, par 4

29. La Costa, Carlsbad, California

30. "Z" hole

31. Robert Trent Jones

32. Steuben Glass

33. Gary Player

34. Sea Pines, South Carolina

35. "The New American Riviera"

36. Innisbrook, Tarpon Springs

37. Championship Island Course, 18th hole, one of the toughest in the U.S.

38. Mike Schmidt

39. Doral Hotel & Country Club

40. The Breakers

41. The Villa Medici in Rome

42. Henry Morrison Flagler

43. The Greenbrier, White Sulphur Springs, West Virginia

44. 1910

45. Jack Nicklaus

46.  Robert Trent Jones

47.  In reference to the adventurous 1716 expedition of Virginia Governor Alexander Spotswood from Williamsburg over the Appalachian mountains. Upon returning to Williamsburg, the Governor presented each member of the expedition with a golden horseshoe. Playing this fine course can be likened to a unique adventure.

48.  Del Snyder

49.  The Woodlands Inn, The Woodlands, Texas (par 5, 545 yards)

50.  Oceanside Course at Sawgrass

51.  Ron Polane, resident golf pro for the Mobil Five-Star, AAA Five-Diamond Boca Raton Hotel and Club